The American Vision of
Robert Penn Warren

William Bedford Clark

The American Vision of
Robert Penn Warren

THE UNIVERSITY PRESS OF KENTUCKY

Scholarly publisher for the Commonwealth,
serving Bellarmine College, Berea College, Centre
College of Kentucky, Eastern Kentucky University,
The Filson Club, Georgetown College, Kentucky
Historical Society, Kentucky State University,
Morehead State University, Murray State University,
Northern Kentucky University, Transylvania University,
University of Kentucky, University of Louisville,
and Western Kentucky University.

Editorial and Sales Offices: Lexington, Kentucky 40508-4008

Library of Congress Cataloging-in-Publication Data

Clark, William Bedford, 1947-
   The American vision of Robert Penn Warren / William Bedford Clark.
       p.   cm.
   Includes bibliographical references (p.   ) and index.
   ISBN 0-8131-1756-9 (acid-free paper)
   1. Warren, Robert Penn, 1905-1989—Political and social views.
2. National characteristics, American, in literature. 3. Social
problems in literature. 4. Politics in literature. I. Title.
PS3545.A748Z653   1991
813'.52—dc20   90-28299

Contents

. . . it was my West, the West I bought and gave and never
Saw, or but like the Israelite,
From some high pass or crazy crag of mind, saw—
I saw all,
Swale and savannah and the tulip-tree
Immortally blossoming to May,
Hawthorn and haw,
Valleys extended and prairies idle and the land's
Long westward langour lifting toward the flaming escarpment
    at the end of the day.
Saw the sad bison lick the outstretched hand,
And on the western rock, wracked in the clang and smother,
The black seal barks, and loves us, knowing we will come.
For wind is steady, and the moon rides gold,
Suns execute their arrogant processional
Of deep delight, and the illimitable glitter
Of distance dazzles to our human fulfillment.
It was great Canaan's grander counterfeit.
Bold Louisiana,
It was the landfall of my soul.

> Thomas Jefferson, in Warren's *Brother to Dragons*
> (1953 version)

Have you ever thought how the moonlit continent
Would look from the tearless and unblinking distance of
    God's wide eye?

> Warren, "Homage to Theodore Dreiser on the
> Centennial of His Birth" (1971)

Shortened and Abbreviated Titles

AHG	Robert Penn Warren, *At Heaven's Gate* (1943; New York: New Directions, 1985)
AKM	Robert Penn Warren, *All the King's Men* (1946; New York: Harcourt Brace Jovanovich, 1982)
BD	Robert Penn Warren, *Brother to Dragons: A Tale in Verse and Voices* (New York: Random, 1953)
DP	Robert Penn Warren, *Democracy and Poetry* (Cambridge: Harvard Univ. Press, 1975)
EP	Robert Penn Warren, *Eleven Poems on the Same Theme* (Norfolk, Conn.: New Directions, 1942)
Image	Daniel Boorstin, *The Image, or What Happened to the American Dream* (New York: Atheneum, 1962)
ITMS	*I'll Take My Stand: The South and the Agrarian Tradition* (1930; reprint, Baton Rouge: Louisiana State Univ. Press, 1977)
JB	Robert Penn Warren, *John Brown: The Making of a Martyr* (New York: Payson & Clarke, 1929)
NR	Robert Penn Warren, *Night Rider* (Boston: Houghton Mifflin, 1939)
Segregation	Robert Penn Warren, *Segregation: The Inner Conflict in the South* (New York: Random, 1956)
SJ	Allen Tate, *Stonewall Jackson: The Good Soldier* (New York: Minton, Balch, 1928)
Talking	Floyd C. Watkins and John T. Hiers, eds., *Robert Penn Warren Talking: Interviews 1950-1978* (New York: Random, 1980)
TSP	Robert Penn Warren, *Thirty-Six Poems* (New York: Alcestis, 1935)

"Use of the Past"	Robert Penn Warren, "The Use of the Past," in *A Time to Hear and Answer: Essays for the Bicentennial Season* (University: Univ. of Alabama Press, 1977)
WET	Robert Penn Warren, *World Enough and Time* (New York: Random, 1950)
WOA	Herbert Agar and Allen Tate, eds., *Who Owns America?* (Boston: Houghton Mifflin, 1936)
WSN	Robert Penn Warren, *Who Speaks for the Negro?* (New York: Random, 1965)

Preface

In 1986, Robert Penn Warren was named the first official poet laureate of the United States. His appointment was at once appropriate and ironic, though the fact was likely lost on all but a few of the members of Congress who confirmed him. To be sure, no American writer of this century was more intrigued by the nation's history nor more susceptible to the sweeping grandeur of its landscape, but by the same token few writers equalled Warren when it came to cataloging the liabilities of America's past and present and assessing the problematic nature of its future. In interviews with representatives of the popular press, Warren made it clear that he accepted the laureateship with the understanding that he would not be called upon to produce works of national commemoration, and yet—for all his uncompromising honesty—Warren had already on more than one occasion celebrated and commended the striking audacity of the Founders' dream. The present study aims at a better understanding of the dynamic tensions that inform Warren's characteristically American vision, and in this respect it may be said to complement two recent books, each excellent in its own way: John Burt's *Robert Penn Warren and American Idealism* (1988) and Hugh Ruppersburg's *Robert Penn Warren and the American Imagination* (1990).

However, I approach Warren's ambivalent relationship with America from a decidedly different perspective. In part, I have endeavored to "historicize" his writing to a degree that has not been attempted thus far, though Leonard Casper made a start in that direction in *Robert Penn Warren: The Dark and Bloody Ground* in 1960. At the same time, I have sought to avoid what I regard as the sometimes pernicious reductivism one finds in the work of many self-proclaimed "new historicists." (As to "ideology," I freely confess that my own "enabling assumptions" are close to those of Warren—though by no means congruent.) While I have taken pains to provide an accurate overview of Warren's achievement, I make no pretense of inclusivity. Warren's career spanned six decades. For my purposes, it has seemed best to bring primary attention to bear on the years 1925 through 1955, for it was over this period that his characteristic vision assumed its clearest focus and sharpest definition. Since I have addressed "The Ballad of Billie Potts," *Brother to Dragons*, and *Audubon* at some length in other contexts, I have resisted the temptation to repeat myself verbatim in these pages. However, it should be noted that my first chapter, in somewhat abbreviated form, did appear in the *Southern Review* (Autumn 1986).

I was honored by the interest Mr. Warren himself showed in this project from its inception and will always appreciate the encouragement he provided me in many ways, great and small. I would likewise express my gratitude to Cleanth Brooks, who graciously extended moral and material support to me at crucial points along the way. Thanks are also due to four distinguished Warren scholars—James H. Justus, Hugh Ruppersburg, Victor Strandberg, and James A. Grimshaw, Jr.—for their varied assistance. The lengthy citations from *Brother to Dragons* (copyright 1953, by Robert Penn Warren) are reprinted by permission of Random House, Inc. I owe special thanks to the William Morris Agency for permission to quote from "Bicentennial," to the Estate of Robert Penn Warren for permission to quote from "Iron Beach" and "To Certain Old Masters," and to John Burt for his generous assistance with permissions. I would also register my gratitude to the College of Liberal Arts at Texas A&M University and Dean Daniel Fallon for their ongoing support. A Travel to Collections Grant from the National Endowment for the Humanities (supplemented by a grant from the Interdisciplinary Group for Historical Literary Study at Texas A&M University) made it possible for me to work with the Warren Papers in the Beinecke Library at Yale. Patricia Willis of the Beinecke staff was most helpful. My valued colleague Jerome Loving read the first four chapters of this book with careful attention to detail and offered several important suggestions, and he was instrumental in securing for me a funded Faculty Development Leave from Texas A&M, without which the completion of my study would have been considerably delayed. My debt to the wisdom, both published and private, of Lewis P. Simpson defies sufficient acknowledgment. By precept and example, he is largely responsible for whatever value my research and writing over the years may claim. Without question, my deepest gratitude belongs to Floyd C. Watkins, who subjected my original manuscript to the most rigorous and tough-minded reading imaginable. I think it fair to say that Professor Watkins would have preferred for me to have written an entirely different kind of book, but it was in fact his frank critique that enabled me to grasp my own purposes more securely and bring my project to a timely closure. No one could ask for a better or more demanding friend.

1

Bicentennial in Babylon

Long before it arrived, 1976, as the bicentennial year, had been designated a time for retrospective contemplation of America's past, an occasion for national self-congratulation and celebration. Nonetheless, the first half of the 1970s had been filled with events that were decidedly inauspicious. For the first time in history, an American president, under threat of almost certain impeachment, had been forced to resign his office (his vice-president had resigned in disgrace some time before), and the bitterly divisive war in Vietnam, the nation's longest, had ended with the pathetic image of abandoned Asians clinging to the struts of the American helicopters that frantically evacuated the U.S. Embassy in Saigon. The American electorate yearned for a fresh start in 1976, and by a narrow margin they turned out the appointed presidential incumbent, Gerald Ford, in favor of Jimmy Carter, the first chief executive from the Deep South since before the Civil War (only to reject him in turn four years later).

In many ways, 1976 *was* a good year for Americans: the unmanned Viking spaceship landed on Mars and sent back dramatic pictures of the Red Planet; Americans, including the novelist Saul Bellow, made a clean sweep of the Nobel Prizes that year; and an engaging young man named Bruce Jenner took the Olympic decathlon. There were other heroes, like the boyish Mark "The Bird" Fidrych, an unlikely, eccentric, but likable Big League pitcher, and champions of America's cultural achievements could take a somewhat ambivalent pride in the long-delayed admission of the expatriate Henry James into the company of Britain's Westminster Abbey immortals. Other signs were clearly less propitious. A granddaughter of William Randolph Hearst was convicted of bank robbery under the most bizarre of extenuating circumstances, and the Lockheed scandals suggested that American business practices involved as a matter of course the corruption of foreign officials.

Allegations of sexual improprieties rocked Congress, and investigations into the FBI and CIA turned up disturbing evidence of the harrassment of private citizens and the systematic violation of their civil rights. Other events were open to varied interpretations. One ruling of the Supreme Court prepared the way for a renewal of capital punishment, and another denied the fathers of unborn children the right to veto a woman's decision to have an abortion. The family of the comatose Karen Anne Quinlan won judicial permission to remove her from life-supporting devices (she lived on nevertheless), and the transsexual Renee Richards made a brief splash on the women's professional tennis circuit. The manufacture, installation, and theft of CB radios became in turn important industries, and Americans owned an estimated 125 million television sets. The popularity of films like *Rocky*, *The Omen*, and the remake of the classic *King Kong* suggested a good deal about the collective American mood, as did the proliferation of singles bars and the fact that sterilization became the fastest-growing form of birth-control. On the West Coast, physicians staged a slowdown to protest malpractice insurance rates, and, in Philadelphia, bicentennial promoters voiced their disappointment that fewer tourists than expected had visited the nation's birthplace in 1976. There were disturbing instances of patronization from abroad as well: the supersonic Concorde, a joint product of British and French technology, was granted permission to cross the Atlantic despite its controversial noise levels; the German firm of Volkswagen made plans to open an assembly plant in the United States; and the Korean evangelist the Reverend Sun Myung Moon announced his intention to sponsor a Bicentennial God Bless America Festival in Yankee Stadium.

As the year came to a close, *Esquire* magazine, itself something of an American institution, published a poem by the nation's preeminent man of letters, Robert Penn Warren. "Bicentennial" hardly represents Warren's best work (he excluded it from subsequent collections of his verse), but it deserves careful study as an index to his feelings as America observed its 200th anniversary of independence. In form it resembles a mosaic, or, more properly, a kind of cinematic montage, yet its disparate fragments somehow assume a cumulative unity that figures forth the fragmentation of our national experience, a shared destiny suggested by the poem's epigraph, the biblical query "Who is my brother?" In seeking to answer that question, Warren begins with a mock vision of apocalypse:

> Wall Street aflame, strategic police stations
> Occupied, the *Times* building a shambles, and
> The mayor assassinated—that
> Is what you might logically assume, with everything
> On four wheels burning rubber over
> Every bridge, heading in every
> Direction, and every
> Public-service thermometer racking up
> Ninety-three degrees, and the pollution
> Quotient inimitable.—But, no,
> Don't worry, it is only
> Another Friday afternoon, and July Fourth
> Looming up.[1]

The evacuation of the city for the holiday weekend is "only an exercise in patriotism" in which each citizen seeks "his own version of Walden Pond," but for Warren such an essentially Transcendentalist quest for self through flight is by its very nature bogus, and "Bicentennial" proceeds to unfold a series of case histories to illustrate symptoms of a national malaise.

The first character we meet, Caleb Winthrop, whose name evokes the pilgrim fathers, is caught up in a travesty of his ancestors' errand into the wilderness as he commutes at the end of the day to his suburban home in Greenwich. Drinking in the bar car only accentuates his inarticulate sense of quiet desperation, and what comfort he later takes in the thought of his macho sexuality as he contemplates his "member" while bathing is self-deceptive, for his alcoholism is gradually rendering him impotent, and his anticipated lovemaking after an obligatory cocktail party ends with his wife "panting" desperately in the dark: "It had started out all right, but then, / No matter what she did, the bastard passed out on her." As "a little light seeps in, past the curtains, / From the stars light-years away," Mrs. Winthrop concentrates her more earthly efforts on a frenetic masturbation. If the case of the Winthrops may be said to represent in part the sad culmination of the New England way, the history of Murdoch Lancaster, who has realized the rags-to-riches myth dear to the American heart, comes quite literally to a dead end. The son of a father who "always smelled of turpentine," Lancaster became a military man and multimillionaire. Now he sits in his Westchester County estate, his only reading American history ("except financial reports"), and meditates on his lost Alabama boyhood. Estranged from his children, with no friend but his black chauffeur, Lancaster has determined with a combination of military resolution, Roman stoicism, and self-defeating illogic that the only proper solution to his wife's cancer is murder-suicide:

> Having done what he has done, Murdoch Lancaster
> Kneels at the foot of his bed. "Now I lay me—"
> He hears his mind saying, as he sets the muzzle
> Between his teeth. With the muzzle there,
> He laughs at his foolish mind.
>
> The muzzle tastes like smoke.

The bicentennial malaise is not, Warren scrupulously shows, confined to the eastern elite, nor to the middle-aged and old. A young black heroin addict in the Bronx suffers from it, and the Winthrops' baby-sitter, in her mindless copulation with a new boyfriend ("She doesn't know him well yet"), differs little except in social caste and geographical location from the bestial Louisiana moss pickers in the poem, whose primal depravity suggests the slimy bedrock of human experience.[2] Meanwhile, the ghetto merchant Moshe Weinstein obsessively pursues his own version of the American Dream in Bridgeport, Connecticut, overcharging his "spade" customers until he himself falls victim in a robbery and loses his life in a vain effort to save the day's receipts. Even the golden future that would seem to await Spike Oleson, a National Merit Scholar bound for Harvard in the fall, is undercut by the knowledge that his future will be paid for in part by the continued hardship of his widowed mother. Though these latter characters are not drawn with the depth and detail that Warren brings to his portraits of Caleb Winthrop and Murdoch Lancaster, their presence in the poem is essential as testimony to the complexity and range of frustration and futility in American life. Indeed, it is easy to agree with Victor Strandberg that "Bicentennial" is in a real sense a parodic response to Whitman,[3] a panoramic overview of a nation less vital than vacuous, and the tragic-comic absurdity of the characters' fates is intensified by a series of interpolated images of the American landscape that reaffirm Warren's genuine love for the physical grandeur of the continent and provide an ironically sublime backdrop for the characters' sordid and pitiable lives.

"Bicentennial" ends with a less than pietistic invocation of the Founding Fathers. These framers of a new nation held forth the promise of "the pursuit of happiness," but, Warren adds, "It is hard to know what happiness is. / They did not tell us." Still, the poet would have Americans remember "the virtues of the old ones who, / Backs to a dark continent, stood and set us free from tyranny." The bottom line, however, is also the poem's last: "They did not get around to setting us free from ourselves."

In this deceptively simple sentence, Warren points toward a dominant thematic tension that informs the entire range of his writing. How do we best assume the threatening burden of our liberty? In a society based on the promise of self-actualization, but subject itself to the exigencies of history and happenstance, how do we become ourselves?

Were we to concentrate on the vacuity that defines the existences of the Americans who people "Bicentennial," it might be tempting to dismiss the poem as little more than the jaundiced grumblings of a man beginning the seventh decade of his life, but to do so would be to ignore the genuine insights embodied in the work and, more important, to misread Warren's passionate commitment to the promise implicit in the American experience. The late Arlin Turner described Mark Twain's relationship to his native South as "An Affair of Love and Anger,"[4] and this same phrase might be productively applied to Warren's relationship to the nation at large. In a televised interview with Bill Moyers during the bicentennial year, Warren made predictably gloomy observations about the conformity and philistinism of the technocratic state, described Watergate as a tragic "melodrama" regrettably come to life, and lamented the "appalling" level of governmental deception that had accompanied the Vietnam War. But the interview began and ended with Warren's emphatic insistence that he was "in love with America."[5] Indeed, early on he expressed that love in a way that startlingly parallels the sentiments of a Carl Sandburg or the manic enthusiasm of a character out of Kerouac: "I've traveled in the Depression in a fifty-dollar car, broken-down, old green Studebaker. I wandered all over the West. I spent time on ranches here and ranches there and have been in all sorts of places. And I've had change given back to me for gas in the Depression. Some guys say, Oh, keep the change buddy; you look worse than I do. I really fell in love with this country" (*Talking* 196).

Warren had high praise as well for the rich heritage of the American past, with all its intrinsic drama, and again his enthusiasm expressed itself unmistakably in the disjointed volubility of his words: "The story is just so goddam wonderful. I mean the whole thing from the . . . the little handful of men, you know, who pledged their lives and sacred honor and set off the world. It's a great story. And it's the plain sweat and pain that went into this country . . . and integrity, that incredible integrity" (*Talking* 208). America's "incredible energy" and "incredible humor" likewise were objects of Warren's enthusiastic commendation, as was the unprecedented complexity of the nation's collective experience, especially as embodied in its folklore: "The whole tale of the . . . the folk tales, incredible number of folk tales, just an incredible number of folk tales.

The whole sense of the . . . the whole Southwest . . . it's incredible. But it's the complexity that is . . . is engaging. But what I hate is they destroy the complexity, to wipe out all that past and see us outside the past like that. I know we've had heroic ages, that it's Homeric" (*Talking* 209).

The frequency with which Warren resorts to the word "incredible" in these passages points toward a residual Adamic wonder in his vision of America, but, to pursue the biblical trope Warren himself suggested in "Knowledge and the Image of Man,"[6] Warren was an Adam who had tasted of the fruit of knowledge. He knew only too well that there were forces at work in America that ran counter to the Founders' dream of a society based on "sacred honor" and "integrity," forces that would cut Americans off from a sustaining sense of the past and erase the vital "complexity" of the nation in favor of a barren homogeneity. Given this state of affairs, the responsibilities of the writer in America are at once agonizing and inescapable. Warren reminds Moyers of the prophetic role novelists like Cooper, Melville, and Faulkner have traditionally assumed in American literature: "It's an extremely critical literature, critical of America and constantly rebuking America and trying to remake it" (*Talking* 217). Clearly, Warren saw himself as a member of this company and a part of this tradition, and his revealing conversation with Moyers not only dramatizes his profound ambivalence toward America, it asserts in no uncertain terms his sense of mission as a man of letters in the new New World.

As early as 1943, in a review of *At Heaven's Gate*, the critic Malcolm Cowley had noted Warren's role as a "social historian," though he was careful to point out that Warren would probably chafe at the suggestion.[7] Still, with proper qualification, Cowley's insight is, as usual, an invaluable one, for it is undeniable that, over the more than half-century in which he wrote, Warren repeatedly addressed himself, both directly and indirectly, to the crucial social issues of his time: the impact of economic injustice, political corruption, racism, war, industrialism, and technology on the individual consciousness. Yet, even in his Agrarian days, Warren's critique of American shortcomings had never been comfortably doctrinaire, no doubt in part as a consequence of his grasp of the intricate and interlocking factors that have shaped American history and defined the nature of the problems Americans face. Indeed, in an altogether positive way, Warren was perhaps the most *self-consciously historical* of modern American writers, though Warren's historical perspective is also informed by a broader philosophical turn of mind that instinctively perceived the exigencies of a given time and place against the backdrop of the perennial questions that have haunted Western thought: How does man know his world and, more important, his self? How does he learn to live with the human fate? Warren's affair of love and anger with America had an inner dimension at its core, and any meaningful exploration of his achievement as a "social historian" must recognize the significance of what he told Edwin Newman in 1971: "Any intelligent person is inclined to criticize his country more strongly than he will criticize anything else. And he should. He should. It's a way of criticizing himself, too. Trying to live more intelligently, and more fully" (*Talking* 159).

When the "intelligent person" in question is a writer, such a critical discipline results in an art that straddles social and psychic realities, for as Warren wrote in "The Veins of Irony," literature "looks out" and "records a world" and "looks in" and "records a man."[8] An important a priori assumption running throughout Warren's work is the essentially Platonic notion that the polis is the individual writ large, and Barnett Guttenberg is right to imply that Warren's "indictment of the modern world" is a corollary to his perennial concern with the alienation and estrangement of the individual from himself,[9] since society and the self, the forces of history and the freedom of the individual will, are inextricably linked in a symbiotic balance in Warren's fictive vision. The author's efforts to define the *was* and *is* of the American experience against what that experience might (and should) be were part of a continuing process of self-definition. To reverse the order of this formula is merely to recast the poles of the dialectic: the compulsion to realize the promise of the fully integrated self corresponds to the challenge to actualize a society in which the dignity of the individual is a given and the integrity of the individuated Self is the principal end. As Warren told Ralph Ellison and Eugene Walter in 1957, "America was based on a big promise—a great big one: the Declaration of Independence . . . When you have to live with that in the house, that's quite a problem—particularly when you've got to make money and get ahead, open world markets, do all the things you have to, raise your children, and so forth. America is stuck with its self-definition put on paper in 1776, and that was just like putting a burr under the metaphysical saddle of America—you see, that saddle's going to jump now and then and it pricks" (*Talking* 40). Shifting his figure of speech somewhat, Warren might have added that the burr of "self-definition" is left to fester most painfully in the hearts of America's writers.

On the broadest level, of course, such juxtaposition of the ideal and the real makes for a universal irony that informs the entire sweep of Western literature, but for Warren that irony seemed peculiarly the province of the American writer by virtue of his nation's theoretical origins. In the *Paris Review* interview with Ellison and Walter cited above, Warren noted with approbation the contention of the nineteenth-century Polish observer Adam Gurowski that while "other nations" were "accidents of geography," America was "based on an idea" (*Talking* 40). For Warren, the formulator of that idea was Thomas Jefferson— scholar, scientist, statesman, and reluctant slave-holder— whose Declaration of Independence was in a sense itself an exercise in self-definition, an attempt to recreate the world in accordance with the Enlightenment's paradoxical passion for reason.[10] The debate between Thomas Jefferson and R.P.W. that dominates the structure of Warren's most ambitious poem, *Brother to Dragons* (1953; revised version, 1979), is merely the most explicit and extensive rendering of a dialogue Warren carried on throughout the course of his career. James H. Justus, one of the best of Warren's commentators, has remarked that "all of Warren's fiction, as well as much of his other work, seems intended . . . to counter Thomas Jefferson's extravagant vision of America as a people 'not chosen to fulfill history but a people freed from history.' " [11] In accordance with his desire to free each new generation from the debts of the fathers, Jefferson may at times have lost sight of what has been called "the laws of historical cost accounting," and nowhere was that failing more fraught with future disaster than in Jefferson's (and his contemporaries') willingness to leave the problem of resolving the question of slavery in the hands of generations of Americans to come. [12] Yet, it should be emphasized that Warren's critique of the Jeffersonian vision, like his critique of America itself, is fundamentally a labor of love.

It was the spirit of Jeffersonian democracy, with all its concern for self-realization, not simply Jeffersonian agrarianism, that lay behind I'll Take My Stand (1930) and Who Owns America? (1936), the two political symposia to which Warren contributed early in his career; and Jefferson's dream of a nation gradually unfolding its destiny westward, manifested in the fact of the Louisiana Purchase, perennially provided Warren with one of his most evocative themes. Warren was fully aware that Jefferson was no naive visionary, as he made clear in Brother to Dragons, [13] but rather a man who recognized that whatever progress mankind may ultimately claim must be paid for through dogged effort. [14] Nor—and this fact is crucial—was Jefferson, for all his devotion to the promise of the future, a man who lacked an informing sense of the past. Warren explored the necessity for just such a historical sense in "The Use of the Past," the Franklin Lecture he delivered at Auburn University in 1973, and, quite significantly, he framed his remarks with an eye toward the looming bicentennial: "My subject tonight is the use of the past. I see the subject in the immediate context of the particular crises of the past two decades—political and cultural—for it seems to me that associated with those crises, sometimes as cause and sometimes as consequence, is a contempt for the past. But also, and more broadly, I see this subject in the context of impending celebration of our second centennial of nationhood." [15] Warren elaborated further: "On July 4, 1876, in an address delivered at Taunton, Massachusetts, Brooks Adams demanded: 'Can we

look over the United States and honestly tell ourselves that all
things are well with us?' And he answered his own question:
'We cannot conceal from ourselves that all things are not well.'
Almost a century later, looking forward to July 4, 1976, one
does not stamp himself as a prophet of doom if he predicts that
on that date we will be forced to echo the answer that Adams
gave to his own question" ("Use of the Past" 3).

However, Warren wonders aloud whether many Americans
"in this age of adman blandness, public-relations images, and
moral ambiguities" will indeed trouble themselves to frame
such a question at all. He cannot deny that when Henry Ford
dismissed the past with a memorable, if brutal, formula ("History is bunk."), he spoke from sentiments buried deep in many
an American heart, yet Warren is quick to remind his audience
that Jefferson, for all his orientation toward the new nation's
future, saw the study of history as a necessary basis for equip-
ping a free citizenry to live in a free society, even though that
society had from its inception professed a "mission" to "make
all things new" ("Use of the Past" 6).

Warren was too realistic, and too fair, a man to suggest that
our nation's ahistorical impulse to free itself from the burden
of time has bred nothing but unmitigated disaster. Indeed,
much of America's greatness must be credited to its collective
faith in the efficacy of new beginnings, as Warren freely admits:

The sense of being freed from the past, of being reborn, of being forever innocent, did give America an abounding energy, an undauntable
self-reliance, and an unquenchable optimism, and we should be lack-
ing in gratitude to Providence to deny these obvious benefits. But
sometimes virtues have their defects, and sometimes, even, the defects tend to run away with the virtues. If, in America, the past was
wiped out and Americans felt themselves to be—to adapt a phrase
from Emerson—the "party of the Future," they also felt themselves to
be a Chosen People, who, unlike the Jews, could never sin in God's
sight. Furthermore, they came to feel that even their whims, ap-
petites, and passing fancies were an index of God's will. ["Use of the
Past" 6-7]

In short, Warren is suggesting that America's strengths carry
within themselves the seeds of tragic failure; unchecked op-

timism, oblivious to the hard lessons of the past, may easily grow into hybris, the pride that precipitates the fall. The "party of the Future's" attendant millennialism and the corresponding conviction that Americans possess a "Hot Line to the Most High" may well manifest themselves as a ruthlessness in the national character, albeit a ruthlessness in the guise of a disinterested pursuit of the greater good. In this connection, Warren's subsequent allusion in his address to the crushing of Filipino resistence at the turn of the century bore an unmistakable, if unstated, relevance to the United States' late debacle in Southeast Asia, for, following Warren's line of reasoning (in which the insights of Reinhold Niebuhr play an acknowledged and formative role), Americans' often uncritical faith in the rightness of their cause belongs among the more dangerous "illusions of our national infancy" ("Use of the Past" 10).

Warren ends his "preamble" with a series of sobering questions: "Are we ready to take our second centennial as an occasion that may, possibly, teach us something? Are we ready to face the idea that we may not, after all, be the Chosen People? Are we ready even to consider the possibility that we are moral narcissists of great talent and are, as a consequence, somewhat unlovely and sometimes unlovable? Are we ready to learn from our past that moral definition is difficult and that there is such a thing as what Niebuhr calls the 'irony of history'?" The necessity of asking ourselves such questions is imperative given the ironies of a historical predicament that means in effect that "what was once our future is now our past," but Warren notes that this cyclical paradox is itself "the deepest irony of all" and one that only a mature national consciousness is prepared to wrestle with ("Use of the Past" 11)

In Warren's view, as he proceeds to articulate it in his Franklin Lecture, a sense of history is of paramount importance, though he discounts the notion that the study of history in and of itself can provide us with tidy solutions to the dynamic problems of the present or insulate us from the risks of making mistakes in the future: "For the future is always full of booby traps, and there is no indication that historians make the best prime ministers, secretaries of state, or even advisors to presidents, kings, and emperors" ("Use of the Past" 16). Rather, the value of history lies in the fact that it provides us with images of humanity in action in the past in a way analogous to the working of literature upon our consciousnesses, and, by internalizing these images, we can come to assimilate the full burden of our humanity. If the past is sometimes a rebuke to the present, it is also the source of a solid foundation upon which to erect the vision of a future, since "the dynamic understanding of the past gives us the possibility of a future" ("Use of the Past" 29).

Underlying Warren's discussion are two premises that are central to his worldview: that the self isolated in time and alienated from the context of community is ultimately non-self and that a genuinely viable selfhood can come only by way of "earned" self-definition. We are called to participation in the world and must subject ourselves to a process of action and interaction with others. What Quentin Anderson has identified as the "imperial self,"[16] a dominant mode of the American imagination, was for Warren anathema, potentially destructive of both the individual who suffers from it and of the society that projects it on a more general level. So it is that the proper sense of the past, while not an absolute cure for the diseases of the self, diseases Warren viewed as especially rampant in our age of scientism and quantitative reductionism, is nonetheless a potent tonic, and it is hardly surprising that Warren sees in the creative act, specifically as embodied in literature, the fullest paradigm for the vital dialectic between the past and the self for which he calls. Like history, literature "gives us an image of the human soul confronting its fate," but that is only half the matter. It also provides an auxiliary "image of how the writer confronts the image of fate that is the work's content" ("Use of the Past" 25). This "doubleness" enables the reader to confront, albeit vicariously, his own fate and confront himself in the very act of such confrontation: "Literature, as Henri Bergson suggests, returns us to ourselves" ("Use of the Past" 26). Or, as Warren puts it a little later, "The truth we want to come to is the truth of ourselves, of our common humanity, available in the projected self of art. We discover a numinous consciousness and for the first time may see both ourselves in the world and the world in us" ("Use of the Past" 28).

In "The Use of the Past," Warren points to two American writers, Hawthorne and Faulkner, who, in wrestling with the burden of their respective regional pasts, gave their countrymen the kind of art that nurtures the evolving self and promotes the formulation of a viable vision of the future. The value of such an achievement is not to be underestimated, for, as Warren, echoing Proverbs, had written elsewhere, "Where there is no vision the people perish."[17] In the words of L. Hugh Moore, "What our society needs most, Warren believes, is a historical myth and an artist to shape it from our native history."[18] To be sure, America is not short on myths, many of which are self-deluding and pernicious, but the mythic vision Warren called for would be based on a realistic grasp of human limitations and a Niebuhrian respect for the ironies of history; it would reflect as well the inner drama of its creator and shaper. Such a myth cannot be the result of dogmatic oversimplification or the pious invocation of self-congratulatory instances of national virtue. It must be based on a painfully honest appraisal of society and self in which the whole truth, however difficult it may be to face, is allowed to emerge on its own terms.

Here it might be well to contrast Warren's approach to the problem of the writer's place in American culture with that of another man of letters for whom the meaning of the American experience was primary, the quintessential poet-as-public-man Archibald MacLeish. In an influential essay "Public Speech and Private Speech in Poetry" (1938), MacLeish argued eloquently for the social significance of poetry. As opposed to the antiseptic and ultimately solipsistic "private speech" that characterized much of the English poetry of the latter part of the nineteenth century, MacLeish extolled the return to "public speech" he saw represented by "modern" poetry, a mode of literary discourse he regarded as parallel to the medium practiced by giants like Dante, Shakespeare, and Milton, who regarded their art as a mode of expression "capable of consequences," a "poetry of action."[19] The proponent of "public speech" would seek to restore poetry, and all of imaginative literature by extension, to its proper place in the common scheme of things; he would recognize the old truth that "poetry was in the world, and the world was in poetry, and a man was better as a poet as he was more deeply and more understandingly and more naturally in the world."[20]

There is little in MacLeish's basic argment with which Warren would have taken issue.[21] Indeed, Warren would say much the same thing, using his own emphases and diction, in essays like "Pure and Impure Poetry" (1943), for example, but, in the final analysis, Warren's and MacLeish's applications of these shared understandings are strikingly different, though both writers devoted much of their best work to an exploration of the same overriding concern: the meaning of the "promise" of America, especially as articulated in Jefferson's Declaration of Independence. A comparison of the two writers and their respective visions is instructive, though two caveats are in order. While MacLeish was the senior (and indeed brought Warren to work at the Library of Congress during World War II), no question of direct influence need arise in considering their respective investigations of the same historical material, since they are hardly alone among American writers in their preoccupation with Jefferson and westward expansion. By the same token, it would be wrong to reduce MacLeish to the role of mere straw man when discussing Warren's admittedly more engaging achievement, for MacLeish and his writings are entitled to a rigorous and sympathetic reevaluation on their own terms that is sadly overdue. Still, a brief look at MacLeish's practice is one of the best ways to understand Warren's art.

In "Frescoes for Mr. Rockefeller's City" (1933), MacLeish contrasted the Jeffersonian dream of a continent subdued and settled by gentle husbandry with the rape of America's natural resources by "Empire Builders" of a different breed, men like Vanderbilt, Morgan, and Mellon. Drawing upon the journals of the Lewis and Clark Expedition in a way that anticipated

Warren's use of like materials in *Brother to Dragons*, MacLeish evoked an image of a virgin continent awaiting the realization of humanity's fullest potential, though the virgin was to be debauched over time by an exploitative mentality that viewed the land not in terms of a life-source but as an easy prey for rapacious financial greed.[22] At the same time, MacLeish took pains to distinguish his criticism of capitalistic excesses from that of social revolutionaries whose Marxism ran equally counter to the spirit of the American Dream, which for Mac-Leish was unswervingly Jeffersonian. Like Warren, MacLeish regarded Jefferson as the prototypal definer of America,[23] and the figure of Jefferson stands as a mighty rebuke to the vices of the modern age in MacLeish's poem "Brave New World" and in the sequence *America Was Promises* (1939). In the latter work, the poet conceded that once Jefferson's faith in Man was left in the hands of fallible men, the promise of America was distorted and largely violated, an assumption that would later underlie Warren's *Brother to Dragons*. But, unlike Warren, MacLeish was unwilling to grant the Nie-buhrian possibility that the dream itself may have been flawed from its inception,[24] and *America Was Promises* con-cludes with a characteristically MacLeishian exhortation to realize the promise of America (in the face of a worldwide Fascist threat) in its pristine purity, however difficult such a realization might be.

For all his "running quarrel with his time,"[25] MacLeish was ultimately an affirmer, though his optimism was often a be-leaguered and embattled one. As late as 1975, in an explicitly bicentennial verse-drama *The Great American Fourth of July Parade*, he reasserted his belief that the Jeffersonian vision of America would somehow reestablish itself and make all things right. Thus, near the end of his life, MacLeish voiced once again the tenets of a liberal democratic creed that had led him into public life in the first place, taking him in time from the Library of Congress to the State Department and the United Nations. The validity of the Jeffersonian dream was an article of secular faith with MacLeish, one he refused to surrender or radically reinterpret in the face of an assault like Niebuhr's, whose *The Irony of American History* MacLeish attempted to refute in a 1952 essay "The Worm at Heart."[26] One consequence was that "public speech" in MacLeish's verse at times failed to rise above the level of patriotic speechmaking, in poems like "The German Girls! The German Girls!" and "Colloquy of the States," for example.

Warren, on the other hand, found in Niebuhr, as we have seen, a confirmation of certain sentiments that had been present in his own thinking almost from the beginning,[27] and this fact, coupled with a visceral aversion to propaganda art in all its forms, however good the cause, accounts in large part for the different way in which Warren went about realizing the poet's public role and practicing the art of "public speech." Warren too would be an affirmer of the American spirit, but the affirmation he offered was qualified by an abiding awareness that the dream of a just and free society rests on the problematic foundation of our all-too-human and fallible selves. As Warren put it in *Democracy and Poetry*, fittingly enough the Jefferson Lecture in the Humanities for 1974:

Perhaps we are, indeed, the Chosen People—and I should like to think that we are. But it is hard work to stay "chosen," and it is harder to scrutinize our situation and ourselves when our chosenness seems to wear a little thin. And hard to realize that there may be no more automatic solutions, even for us. This is not pessimism. It is, rather, optimism—in the sense that it implies confidence in our will to be, not victims, but makers, of our history. But that optimism implies, too, that we must try to look at ourselves, to recognize that we are not free from the hazards of selfhood, nor of time. (55)

The range of Warren's work, in poetry, fiction, and historical and social commentary, is a vibrant response to the promise of America, but a response chastened by an awareness that, being merely human, we often promise ourselves more than we can deliver—or have bargained for.

In 1966, Warren remarked to an interviewer that "troublous times are the best times to write of but the worst to write in" (*Talking* 85). To be sure, the twentieth century has had more than than its share of troubles, and they have left their indeli ble mark on Warren's writing, even when he turned to earlier periods for his subjects. Warren was born at a time when the United States was making its first clear emergence as a world power. Within his lifetime, America fought a war to make the world safe for democracy, enjoyed the false promise of the 1920s boom, suffered through an economic depression that seemed to call into question the very survival of Western institutions, engaged in a Second World War that dwarfed the first, entered the Atomic Age, saw a not-altogether-bloodless revolution take place in the area of race relations, and experienced the first military defeat in the life of the Union (if we exclude the South's defeat in the Civil War). These decidedly "troublous times" form the backdrop for Warren's achievement; they are, indeed, an inescapable element in the context out of which that achievement was generated. The chapters that follow are a reading of Warren's work in the light of this fact. They progress more or less chronologically, in keeping with Warren's insistence that "the books that I have written, for better or worse, are a record of the various kinds of images of man that I have had at different times" (*Talking* 139).

As we have seen, the creative process for Warren was a continuing exercise in self-discovery, a testing of values and assumptions against the resistant facts of the world. Though Warren's values and assumptions proved to be remarkably consistent over the course of his career, his was hardly the "foolish consistency" Emerson inveighed against. In some instances, in Warren's approach to the race question, for example, his ideas underwent a profound reevaluation, but, even when we find Warren taking what appears to be congruent stands on an issue early and late in his life, a closer look serves to reveal the subtle but real evolution that has transpired. In this respect, Warren resembles that uniquely American thinker William James, who likewise distrusted easy answers, denied the notion of a "block universe," and looked upon self-awareness as a matter of process and potential, not as a kind of psychic stasis.[28] In testing his own experience as a writer in modern America, Warren tested the

American experience itself, and what emerged from his labors is a vision of the meaning of America's past and present that warrants our own thoughtful response, that seeks to engage us in the pursuit of a freedom at which the Founding Fathers could only hint.

2

A 1920s Apprenticeship

To Frederick Lewis Allen, impatient to chronicle the decade or so that had only recently come to a close in 1930, the period from the Armistice to the Great Crash already had the look of "a distinct era in American history."[1] Indeed, even today the Twenties seem to exist in a kind of splendid isolation. Woodrow Wilson's hopes for a new world order emerging from Versailles had been dashed, and at home Prohibition was a legal, though hardly effectual, reality. The Republicans were in, bringing with them prosperity and the promise to keep America free from burdensome foreign entanglements, but there was also Teapot Dome. If for many the 1920s were an age of frantic self-indulgence, of gin-mills, flappers, jazz bands, and the Charleston, these years were also marked by a full measure of troubled self-consciousness as many Americans brooded over, as well as brandished, the jargon of a reductive Freudianism and the automobile and radio gradually but inexorably shrank away the immense distances of the continent.

Writers from abroad, most notably D.H. Lawrence, came to the New World in quest of an elusive, however often berated, vitality the Old World seemed to have lost, while newly confirmed nativists like the William Carlos Williams of *In the American Grain* (1925) displayed an obsessive concern with resurrecting, naming, and re-naming the mythic roots of an identifiably American past. To be sure, many younger writers fled for a time to the Old World, following the precedent of an earlier generation of expatriates like Gertrude Stein and Ezra

Pound, but in doing so they, like their predecessors, merely succeeded in bringing their own experience as Americans into sharper relief, consciously or otherwise. Meanwhile, the forces of the new transatlantic modernism were being felt in New Mexico as well as in Greenwich Village, and a vital new literature was asserting itself on the midwestern prairies, in the nightspots of Harlem, and in the narrow streets of the French Quarter. More to the immediate point, after the Armistice, an unassuming group of faculty and students at Vanderbilt University, several of whom had been called away by the war, recommenced their weekly meetings to discuss philosophy and poetry, and in 1922 they were to publish one of the most significant little magazines of the decade. Two years later, these "Fugitives" officially counted among their number a gawky young undergraduate from Guthrie, Kentucky—"Red" Warren.

Here is not the place to recount the details of the Fugitives' early association and the founding of their magazine of verse. That intriguing tale has been told and retold elsewhere, albeit with varying degrees of success.[2] Still, though the leading lights of the group, John Crowe Ransom, Donald Davidson, and Allen Tate, were by the end of the decade to address themselves to political and social issues in a decidedly committed way, there remains a general misimpression that their work on the *Fugitive* was almost exclusively motivated by aesthetic concerns and largely removed in spirit from the sensibility that informed their subsequent activism. A closer look at the poetry that graced the *Fugitive* during the course of its relatively brief run (1922-1925) is, however, itself sufficient to qualify so persistent an assumption, for several of the better poems to appear in the magazine's pages were, for all their predictably youthful weltschmerz, bookish allusions, and (occasionally genuine) ironic wit, firmly grounded in the promisingly vital, if confused and troubled, social consciousness of the 1920s. It is too easy to overestimate the insularity of Nashville in 1922—the year the first issue of the *Fugitive* rolled off a black-owned press—to the extent of failing to note that the same year saw the coming to power of Mussolini in Italy and the formal creation of the USSR. Nor should we forget that

1922 saw the appearance of Eliot's *The Waste Land* and the first production of Eugene O'Neill's *The Hairy Ape*, two influential testaments to the alienation of the individual psyche in an industrial age, as well as the publication of Cummings's *The Enormous Room*, Fitzgerald's *The Beautiful and the Damned*, and Lewis's *Babbitt*, each in its own way a provocative expression of American literary sensibility in the wake of the Great War.[3]

Admittedly, there is little direct mirroring of the real world in evidence among the early pieces Warren contributed to *Driftwood Flames*, published by the Nashville Poetry Guild in 1923. The ingenuousness of "Wild Oats" is fully in keeping with the tenor of "The Golden Hills of Hell," a poem out of Keats and Poe by way of the Pre-Raphaelites. Whatever apocalyptic sensibility lay behind "The Fierce Horsemen" ("Pitiless, pitiless spoilers, / Raiding the weeping land")[4] soon lost itself in the safe abstraction of seasonal myths. Nevertheless, the painful earnestness of the young Warren's sense of poetic vocation expressed itself unmistakably, if clumsily, in "To Certain Old Masters":

> I have read you and read you, my betters,
> Vivisected every page;
> I have diagnosed even the letters,
> Pent each hell in its private cage.
>
> I have hacked you all into pieces
> And stuck you together again,
> But my questioning round never ceases:
> No solution at all will you deign.
>
> I have seen the man in his volume,
> (I'm as much of a man as you)
> But in spite of all my logic,
> One plus one not always makes two.
>
> I have asked you all how it happened.
> I have questioned you one by one,
> And each of you pettily jealous,
> Feared to tell how the thing was done.
>
> I have prayed but a crumb of your power,
> But a farthing from you all,

> And you gave but a cryptic silence
> From your shelves along the wall.[5]

And so on after the same fashion. The frustrated novice finally consoles himself with the thought that these "old masters" exist only in the crumbling pages of their "dead" books consigned to the wall, while he may yet partake of the inspiration afforded by natural beauty at first hand—undeniably Emersonian sentiments that seem rather surprising coming from the pen of a young man who was soon to voice a pronounced enmity toward New England Transcendentalism.

Despite the testimony of "To Certain Old Masters," both in form and in content, Warren had, even before he reached his twentieth birthday, profited immensely from his insistent study of older masters, as well as from immediate models like Ransom and Tate. This is clear from his wholly creditable performance in the opening of the first of his *Fugitive* poems, "Crusade":

> We have not forgot the clanking of grey armors
> Along the frosty ridges against the moon,
> The agony of gasping endless columns,
> Skulls glaring white on red deserts at noon;
> Nor death in dank marshes by fever,
> Flies on bloated bodies rotting by the way,
> Naked corpses on the sluggish river,
> Sucked from the trampled rushes where they lay.[6]

These lines already point toward the macabre images of death and decay that were to become a veritable signature in the poems of Warren's early maturity.[7] Perhaps even more significant is the fact that "Crusade," despite its medievalism, presents a grandiose historical undertaking in terms of an archetypal quest that ends in dissolution and disappointment. In time, in works like "The Ballad of Billie Potts," *World Enough and Time,* and *Brother to Dragons*, this same quest would be specifically identified with America's westering impulse, and, in the first of the "Three Poems" in the April 1924 *Fugitive,* the geographical (and spiritual) course of American empire is already evoked, the sonnet's fanciful arctic backdrop notwithstanding:

Beyond this bitter shore there is no going,
This iron beach, this tattered verge of land;
Behind us now the tundra dims with snowing,
In front the seas leap crashing on the strand.
Faintly the sun wheels down its quickened arc
While at our backs with inexorable motion
Earth swings forgotten cities into dark
And night sweeps across the polar ocean.

This place has its own peace, assuredly.
Here we, once waked by tramcars in the street,
Shall rest in unperturbed austerity,
Hearing the surf interminably beat,
Watching the pole star overhead until
The arctic summer brings the carrion gull.[8]

Likewise, an important bond that links the youthful poet with his nameless alter ego in the Baudelairean "To a Face in the Crowd" is the fact that both are descended from "an ancient band / Broken between the mountains and the sea."[9] Warren would later spell out the referents of these lines in no uncertain terms when he would adopt much the same language to suggest the epic groping of the American nation westward in work after work.

Louis D. Rubin, Jr., has written that "almost nothing of [Warren's] passion for history . . . gets into the early work."[10] To the contrary, the "passion" was there from the beginning, though abstracted from the density of specific facts. Coupled with it was a predilection, nurtured by Eliot and Pound by way of Tate, to juxtapose the vitality and vigor of a heroic past with the ennui and emptiness of an emasculate present, as in "After Teacups," a mannered, studiedly Prufrockian piece in which Warren seems almost to be taking up the Poundian challenge of rendering the bedrock substance of a Henry James novel through the economy of verse. "Midnight" is yet another poem that pursues a similar strategy, and in these early pieces in which the past is summoned up as a stark rebuke to the present Warren weaves his personal variations on a favorite rhetorical ploy of Tate in such *Fugitive* lyrics as "First Epilogue to Oenia" and, somewhat later, in mature poems like "Aeneas at Washington" (1933). The point is forever the same: the times, as mirrored in the formerly most meaningful of human relationships, are painfully out of joint.

If, as many readers find, the allusiveness of Warren's early verse reveals undeniably the "academic" nature of the young man's muse, this fact should in no way obscure an even more seminal aspect of his creative resources already in evidence. In "Sonnets of Two Summers," it is the physical landscape of the upper South—not the salons of disaffected expatriates in Europe—that is evoked with an almost imagistic clarity. The incipient fictionist's eye for detail and evocative powers of description are present even at this point in his novitiate, and in Warren's *Fugitive* poems about the Dodd family and "Alf Burt, Tenant Farmer" are the seeds of a sympathetic empathy with the everyday lives of southern rural folk that would soon inform Warren's first successful venture into fiction, the short story "Prime Leaf."[11] An even more intriguing cultivation of native materials characterizes "Easter Morning: Crosby Junction," in which the naive piety of a country sermon offers its implicit indictment of the self-crippling canker of twentieth-century skepticism. However much the man of modern sensibility may yearn for a sustaining faith, such grace is long in coming.[12] John L. Stewart may well be right in observing that Warren's brief studies in California and subsequent stays at Yale and Oxford helped to bring the literary potential of indigenous southern materials to the fore in his work,[13] but it is nevertheless clear that as early as the mid-1920s Warren was already beginning to explore the possibilities of his own version of what Faulkner termed a "little postage stamp of native soil."[14]

The former Fugitives first made their role as social critics manifest with the publication of *I'll Take My Stand*, a loosely-knit collection of position papers that followed closely on the heels of the Great Crash. The title, taken from the Confederate anthem "Dixie," and the blatantly regional attribution of authorship ("by Twelve Southerners") effectively localized the perspective from which the symposium's critique of industrial capitalism and technological progress was launched, just as Warren and Tate had feared.[15] Even today, friend and foe alike insist on reading *I'll Take My Stand* as a peculiarly regional document, an un-Reconstructed, perhaps more rhetorical than realistic, reaction to the demon of northern industrialism. Yet, despite Ransom's attempt to bring a consistent order to bear on the volume's disparate offerings through the inclusion of an introductory "Statement of Principles," it was ultimately an aversion to what was happening in America in the late 1920s rather than any shared veneration of the Old South per se that finally unified the respective authors' indictment of the path American democracy seemed to have taken. After all, the strengths of the aristocratic southern way as Stark Young conceived of them had little in common with the yeoman virtues Andrew Lytle chanted. The common denominator, as revealed in Ransom's insistence that the "true" communists were "the Industrialists themselves,"[16] was a concern with maintaining a viable sense of selfhood in the face of a leveling conformity born of mass production and an economy that abstracted labor from its proper orientation toward the soil.

For Ransom, this meant that "modern man" had lost "his sense of vocation" (*ITMS* xlii). While he was willing to concede that industrialism was "the contemporary form of pioneering," Ransom nevertheless insisted that it was a "pioneering on principle, and with accelerating speed" (*ITMS* 15), goal-less and unguided. In "A Mirror for Artists," Donald Davidson decried what he regarded as the creative intellect's unavoidable alienation in such a world, and Allen Tate, in his "Remarks on the Southern Religion," likewise assumed that scientism and its technological accoutrements tended to undermine anything like a holistic sense of mankind's collective past. By contrast, he wrote that "more concrete minds may be said to look at their history in a definite and now quite unfashionable way. They look at it as a concrete series that has taken place in a very real time—by which I mean, without too much definition, a time as sensible, as full of sensation, and as replete with

accident and uncertainty as the time they themselves are living in, moment by moment" (*ITMS* 160). Just such a historical
awareness, a conviction that we may see ourselves in the past,
becomes a persistent assumption in Warren's writings, and
there are other passages scattered throughout *I'll Take My
Stand* that furnish a gloss on Warren's own theories and practice. Davidson's remark that "New England idealism failed in
the debacle of the Civil War that it egged on" (*ITMS* 48), for
example, would eventually be realized with unforgettable dramatic force in Warren's *Band of Angels*, published in 1955, and
be echoed again as late as *Jefferson Davis Gets His Citizenship
Back* in 1980. More important, perhaps, was Tate's assertion
that the modern age tended to divide the human psyche into
two mutually destructive halves, "a self-destroying naturalism
and practicality, on the one hand, and a self-destroying mysticism, on the other" (*ITMS* 163). Warren's greatest fictional
achievement, *All the King's Men*, would reflect precisely this
same tragic dialectic in terms of "the terrible division of [the]
age." [17]

When Tate repeated the phrase "self-destroying" in the passage just cited, he was reinforcing the Agrarians' ultimate
concern with realizing and maintaining a balanced and sound
psychic health within the individual. Indeed, it seems fair to
argue that the contributors to *I'll Take My Stand* were finally
celebrating the external trappings of southern civilization at
once as manifestations of such an inner state of grace and as
bulwarks against its threatened dissolution. [18] The Agrarians
refused to accept what had become the virtually unchallenged
tenet of much of the best American literature from the early
nineteenth century on—that the claims of the self and of the
society at large were forever at odds—and the real radicalism
of their message stemmed from their premise that an integrated sense of selfhood depended upon an organically unified
community and vice versa. For them, society and the self were
mutually interdependent. A society might thus nurture, as
well as maim, the fragile evolving self, just as the degree of
inner stability which characterized an individual citizen,
taken collectively, would inexorably reveal itself in the broader

realm of social institutions for better or for worse. An awareness of how central this notion was to the Agrarian vision adds
a special significance and force to a remark Warren made at
the Fugitives Reunion in 1956: "I thought we were trying to
find—in so far as we were being political—a rational basis for
a democracy."[19]

Note the characteristically Warrenesque emphasis upon
process here—"we were trying to find." If we read Warren's
own contribution to *I'll Take My Stand*, "The Briar Patch," as a
process piece, the best effort of a decidedly youthful Rhodes
Scholar from Kentucky to grapple with the as yet unsettled
problem of racial justice, we need not waste much time in
denouncing a position that in retrospect seems indefensible
and can concentrate on the essay's importance in terms of
Warren's subsequent assumptions about the symbiotic relationship between the self and the community that alone makes
self-definition possible.[20]

Perhaps the most striking thing about "The Briar Patch" is its
author's unswerving assumption that the fates of black and
white southerners alike are inextricably intertwined. Both are
heirs, for good or ill, of a shared past, and from the beginning
Warren is emphatic about black Americans' stake in the democratic experiment: "They might be mobbed from their farms in
Ohio or be forced to spend their days in the cotton-fields under
a blazing Mississippi sun, but America, after all, was home"
(*ITMS* 246). Under slavery—and admittedly Warren was not
disposed to catalogue its familiar horrors—the black man had
had his narrowly circumscribed place in the social fabric
defined for him. With emancipation and enfranchisement, he
was presented with the problematic challenge of finding a
new place for himself, "and the attempt to find it is the story of
the negro since 1865" (*ITMS* 247). Here again, the emphasis is
upon exploration and discovery, and success, Warren maintains throughout his essay, hinges upon the feasibility of self-
definition.

Regardless of the quibbling one may engage in with respect
to certain of Warren's assumptions about the advantages of

slavery, the infamy of Reconstruction, and the necessity of racial segregation, one must admit that, unlike many progressivist commentators of the time, Warren recognized that it was the black American's responsibility to carve out his place in American life, not merely the white man's burden. Warren accorded the black race a willingness and ability to determine its own future that few reformers outside the black community have been prone to allow.[21] For Warren, even at this early stage in his career as a student of American democracy, it was clear that the black man was first and last a human being, and therefore heir to all the psychic frailty that delimited the human fate. Any genuine freedom he might enjoy would have to be paid for by an inner, as well as external, political and social struggle. It could never be the free gift of well-meaning, frequently condescending whites. They had failed, as history had shown, time and again, and their failure, Warren implied, was itself altogether human.

It is in this spirit that Warren applauded Booker T. Washington's suggestion that black and white Americans could " 'be as separate as the fingers, yet one as the hand in all things essential to mutual progress' " (*ITMS* 254). It is also important to note that Warren refused to accept the premise that an elite of black professionals, W.E.B. DuBois's "talented tenth," represented in and of itself an amelioration of the race's marginal status within the American experiment. What was called for was what a later generation would call "Black Pride," an individual's sense of his or her worth as a "negro" *and* a human being.[22] White Americans, especially in the South, faced a parallel challenge: they could only respect themselves as human beings to the extent that they were prepared to grant their black counterparts a full measure of humanity.

Thus, Warren devalues the capacity of industrial progress to solve the plight of blacks in the South. To suppose that generations of racial injustice can be wiped away by the logic of the marketplace is an "exorbitant act of faith" (*ITMS* 255), for in the capitalistic scheme of things the black man is a mere integer in an economic strategy to enhance maximum profits by threatening to interdict the power of white labor to organize. With the tough-minded, pragmatic clarity that so disturbed Donald Davidson,[23] Warren refused to blame black Americans for playing the hand history had dealt them:

No blame is to be attached to the negro himself if his mere presence swells a stockholder's dividends at the expense of a white workman, or if he takes that white workman's job in time of strike. There is no good reason why he should fight the white man's battles if at the same time there is no proper provision for him in the system. In 1919 at the Atlantic City Convention the struggle to gain equal protection for the negro in the American Federation of Labor was won; at least, it was won on paper. But there is a vast difference between that paper victory and a workable system that would embody its principles. [*ITMS* 257]

In light of the last half-century, Warren's assumption that the best hope for a solution to the nation's racial problem lay in the black American's willingness to work out his destiny on the farm and in the small town seems ingenuous, a fact few readers today fail to note. His later investigations into the "race question," *Segregation* (1956) and *Who Speaks for the Negro?* (1965), nonetheless amply demonstrate how fully his deep personal concern with the issue was modified and rethought in accordance with the political and social realities of American racial relations as they steadily, if at times violently, evolved. These differences in the author's attitude and level of sophistication will be dealt with later in the course of this study. What should be stressed here is the common thread that runs throughout Warren's thinking about race and "freedom" in the fullest sense of the word. No set of social circumstances, however propitious, can be depended upon to assure self-actualization. The most debilitating tyranny is that of the insular and misdirected self, a tyranny that enslaves men and women without respect to the color of their skins.

In a short story published in the mid-1930s, "Her Own People," Warren was to explore certain of the premises of "The Briar Patch" with dramatic force. The central irony of that work is that both black and white characters fail to recognize the angst of the servant Viola for what it is: a manifestation of a universally human, not merely racial, malaise. Twenty years later, Warren would devote an entire novel, *Band of Angels*, to the puzzling out of this same problem presented in terms of racial metaphors, and throughout his later fiction and poetry black characters would appear and reappear as shadowy alter egos of white protagonists, dark foils whose alienation implicitly drew the inner inadequacies of their white counterparts in bold relief.[24] Warren's contribution to *I'll Take My Stand* does indeed stand out as something of an anomaly when placed side by side with the efforts of the other contributors. Already his approach to critiquing social ills was tied to the inner struggles of the psyche to an extent that Ransom, Tate, Davidson, and the others could not quite fathom. This is hardly surprising when we recall that he had dwelt at book-length on the vagaries of the dissociated self in *John Brown: The Making of a Martyr* (1929) even before he accepted his assignment to address himself to the question of the black race's place in American society in the Agrarian symposium.

Warren's critics have never reached a consensus on the value of *John Brown*—which might be expected when we consider the degree to which his subsequent books have provoked divided assessments.[25] Nevertheless, one early reviewer, who would become in time a very distinguished historian, praised *John Brown*'s author for taking a balanced view of his subject and was to maintain a solid respect for the biography over the years.[26] That Warren's first book is still capable of eliciting the kind of negative response it does from Harold Bloom, an enthusiast of the later poetry, is ironic testimony to its residual power.[27] Obviously a springboard to Warren's later work, *John Brown* is much more than that. It offers us vivid testimony to the extent to which Warren had evolved a characteristic way of coming at American history from the very outset of his career.[28] To understand fully the achievement represented by *John Brown* and to appreciate the angle of vision it brings to bear upon the American experience, it is necessary to determine what the book is *not*. It is most decidedly not a neo-Confederate biography along the lines of Tate's *Stonewall Jackson* and *Jefferson Davis* or Andrew Lytle's thesis-ridden but eminently readable *Bedford Forrest and His Critter Company*. Like "The Briar Patch," *John Brown* is apprentice work, but apprentice work that declares its author's independence from his supposed mentors and his determination to eschew prefabricated "truths" in favor of exploring the often perplexing complexity of the human predicament as embodied in the naked, frequently contradictory and unsatisfying, facts of history. Warren may indeed have begun with notions of debunking a martyred abolitionist hero, but in the end he presents a portrait of Brown that stubbornly resists facile schematization.

Tate's two biographies stand in sharp contrast, in part because he wrote them with an agenda in mind.[29] Of the two, *Stonewall Jackson* is the lesser, a kind of un-Reconstructed southern hagiography, in style and substance almost a boy's book. The opening account of Jackson's childhood is worthy of Parson Weems (who is, indeed, alluded to in the text), and Tate insists upon his subject's unswerving morality and fixity of will from the outset. Tate's young Stonewall is a cloying composite of Honest Abe (reading borrowed books) and Tom Sawyer (stripped of mischief and humor). In time the boy fathers a man whose character, Tate would have us believe, is reducible to a formula: "Jackson was one of those distinguished persons whose ambition is so far-reaching that a single object, outside themselves, cannot contain it. The impulse is thrown back upon itself; not the achievement of a simple end, but the exercise of character for its own sake, becomes the unconscious aim of such men. It is the paradox of the great that the most ambitious are the most disinterested. Thomas Jackson was one of these."[30]

Tate notes that "Jackson's character was, with respect to will, overdeveloped; he was a moral Procrustes" (*SJ* 194), but he presents this ultimately unflattering quality of his hero with unqualified approbation, evidence of a simplicity of selfhood that dissociated Modern Man might well envy. Stonewall is Tate's version of Nietzsche's *Übermensch*, a man whose strength of personality was fixed long before he entered West Point, fought in Mexico, taught mathematics at the Virginia Military Institute, and assumed command of the Stone-wall Brigade. Yet, despite Tate's eulogizing of this "great, simple man" (*SJ* 279), he mentions in passing, but pointedly ignores, aspects of Jackson's career and personality that force-fully suggest that the soldier-hero was anything but "sim-ple" and self-contained. What of Jackson's hypochondria and propensity for "obscure" complaints? What of the im-plicit tendency toward alcoholism revealed in Jackson's re-marks that he "always liked" strong drink—" 'That's why I let it alone. I fear it more than the Yankees' bullets' " (*SJ* 225)? Were there not hints of manic hysteria in Jackson's behavior following the Southern victory at First Manassas: "While the Yankees were retreating over the Stone Bridge, Jackson went to his surgeon. As Major McGuire dressed his wound, Jackson, jerking his head excitedly, kept saying: 'Give me 10,000 men and I will be in Washington tomorrow morn-ing.' " (*SJ* 90)?

Tate dutifully acknowledges Jackson's inexplicable behav-ior during the Seven Days fighting; it was "peculiar," Tate admits, but he declines to pursue the matter in depth, and Jackson's bizarre comportment is soon overshadowed by Tate's insistence that Stonewall was a man of inflexible single-mindedness. Most disturbing, perhaps, is Tate's determined preference for Jackson's monomaniacal religiosity (and a concomitant willingness to shed blood) over the balanced re-straint of the more morally circumspect Lee, who drew dis-tinctions between "war" and outright "massacre": "Like every complex sensibility, [Lee] was subject to intuitions that dis-turbed his vision. . . . Up to certain limits he could pursue it with a single purpose. But his character, unlike his great subor-dinate's, was not in any respect overdeveloped. He saw every-thing. He was probably the greatest soldier of all time, but his greatness as a man kept him from being a completely suc-cessful soldier. He could not bring himself to seize every means to the proposed end. Jackson, who saw one object only, could use them all" (*SJ* 272-73).[31]

In his contribution to *I'll Take My Stand*, Tate would une-quivocally propose that the genuinely religious mind was typified by a wide field of vision that refused to substitute a reductive abstractionism for the complexities of the real, "concrete" world. Yet, in *Stonewall Jackson* he condescends to Lee in order to glorify a man who in very many ways resembles Warren's later portrait of John Brown: fanatical, ruthless, a triumph of self over scruples and pride over principle. How do we explain this need on Tate's part to confine the intriguing mystery that was Stonewall Jackson within so tight and distorting a mold? One answer would seem to lie in Tate's suggestion at the end of his *I'll Take My Stand* essay that the contemporary southerner had best take hold of his eroded tradition "through violence" (*ITMS* 174). If Tate were to summon up the life and death of Jackson as a resource against all the modern ills the Agrarians sought to engage in battle, he would have to do so through a decisive exercise of will, by becoming as single-minded and unswerving as Stonewall himself. Ironically, in doing so, Tate fell necessary victim to yet another brand of that very abstract reductionism he feared and abhorred in his better moments—as a writer and as a man—and this same surrender of the complexities of history in pursuit of a manageable ideality is manifest in his biography of Jefferson Davis too.

As its full title, *Jefferson Davis: His Rise and Fall*, suggests, Tate's study of the Confederate president is conceived along the lines of conventional tragedy,[32] and thus Tate works with a ready-made literary formula within which he merely has to arrange the relevant facts of history. The "tragedy" of Davis is at once Aristotelian and Hegelian. High-minded and pragmatic in only the most naive sense, Tate's Davis is in many ways more admirable than his counterpart and nemesis Lincoln, but he is guilty of a pride that makes compromise distasteful and breeds a contempt for lesser men. At the same time, he is a self divided against itself, reluctantly conducting a civil war while torn with an inner division that pits intellect against emotion. Explicitly described by turns as a Hamlet and an Oedipus, Tate's Davis is something of a Coriolanus as well. Reduced to a formulaic equation early on, Tate's Davis never wanders appreciably from it: "He seemed to lack emotional subtlety; while of every logical and intellectual subtlety he was the master. His gaunt ascetic face and withdrawn eyes betrayed a haughty pride." Davis "would expect ideas to settle the course of events, and not quite grasp the necessity of cajoling men into sharing his desires." He was a "great statesman, perhaps the most distinguished statesman in American history," but "he seemed too remote and uncompromising to be a politician."[33]

By the war's conclusion, the man from Mississippi is little more than a deterministic bundle of factors spun from character and adverse circumstance, an "automaton" or a "machine,"[34] who cannot react with anything resembling the freedom of the will. (Here Tate arrives at his version of the theory of the Great Twitch that Warren's Jack Burden pointedly moves beyond in *All the King's Men*.) By the time Tate had finished his two biographies, he was ready to commit himself (albeit only for a time) to a course of action, *political* action of a sort, and like most ideologues he had turned to history for validation of his premises. The South, the last bulwark of European, civilized values, had lost out because of a lack of will. Jackson had had it in spades, but destiny removed him prematurely from the field of play. Davis was tragically flawed, and his tragedy was not only that of the Confederacy but of the modern world as Tate conceived of it.

Tate's "Agrarian" biographies are thesis books. Warren's account of the ambiguous career of John Brown, in spite of the youthful author's unabashed biases, is something more—an evolving meditation on history.[35] Like Tate's subtitles, that of Warren's book, *The Making of a Martyr*, gives us an invaluable clue to the author's intentions. Tate takes the facts of history and constructs an image of the Good Soldier or the Tragic Statesman respectively; Warren is involved in a reversal of that process. He calls upon the testimony of the past to counter, rather than foster, a myth. If the beginning of *Stonewall Jackson* recalls Parson Weems, the opening of *John Brown*—an account of the events leading up to the martyrdom of a spurious ancestor of Brown's in 1511—is indebted to the Renaissance English drama that was to prove a vital influence on Warren

throughout his career. Indeed, at times Warren's Brown behaves remarkably like a stage Machiavell, but he is never
allowed to become one. Warren is finally not disposed merely
to substitute one mythopoeic reading of his protagonist for
another.[36] Instinctively, he goes after bigger game, and the real
John Brown is a most elusive quarry. In his poem "The Por-
tent," Herman Melville had noted that behind the mask (or
hangman's "cap") of Brown was "the anguish none can
draw." Warren would strike through the mask. If in the end
Warren failed to solve completely the human enigma that
was Old Osawatomie, his very failure was an eloquent witness to the ambitious nature of his vision and offered an
undeniable promise of greater things to come. That Warren,
with Tate's patronage,[37] contracted to write a biography of a
celebrated yet infamous abolitionist idol at the threshold of
his career seems in retrospect almost providential. Implicit
in his handling of his subject and his approach to it are
many of the novels, poems, stories, and essays of the next
five decades.[38]

As if his book itself were not sufficient to convey its author's
intentions, Warren makes a point of spelling out the purpose of
his study in no uncertain terms in the "Bibliographical Note"
with which the volume concludes. He faults two of his predecessors, Oswald Garrison Villard (grandson of the abolitionist
William Lloyd Garrison) and Hill Peebles Wilson, for failing to
address themselves in a satisfactory way to the lethal paradox
that was John Brown. Villard was intent upon salvaging whatever glory for Brown he could, in spite of the ultimately damn-
ing testimony his meticulous scholarship had unearthed,
while Wilson, in his furious attempt to demolish a man he had
once admired, was blind to the possibility that Brown may
have been more than a self-serving scoundrel. Both biogra-
phers had overlooked "one of the most significant keys to John
Brown's career and character; his elaborate psychological
mechanism for justification which appeared regularly in
terms of the thing which friends called Puritanism and enemies called fanaticism."[39] Brown was sincere in his crusade
against slavery and anything but a coward, but he was "still

the same man who shot a fine sheepdog" because it was more devoted to someone else, the same man who "embezzled" money from business partners and "slaughtered and stole in Kansas" (*JB* 446). In short, Brown was a bundle of contradictions who challenges our understanding, but just such an "understanding," Warren submits, "is the final aim of this book" (*JB* 447).

One clear index to Brown's elusive complexity is the fact that he earned both the grudging admiration of his foes and the belated condemnation of former allies. Governor Henry Wise of Virginia, who denied all appeals for clemency and thus sent Brown to the gallows at Charlestown, said following Brown's capture at Harper's Ferry: "He is a man of clear head, of courage, fortitude, and simple ingenuousness. He is cool, collected, and indomitable, and it is but just to say that he was humane to his prisoners. . . . He is a fanatic, vain and garrulous, but firm, truthful, and intelligent" (*JB* 392). George Gill, who rode with Brown for a time and occupied a position of importance in Brown's projected Provisional Government, recalled his former chief as "superstitious"and "very selfish and very intolerant." All potential rivals "went down before" Brown's "imperial self." Gill added, "Nothwithstanding claims to the contrary, he was essentially vindictive in his nature" (*JB* 349). Early in life, Brown evinced a profound aversion to firearms; later, at Pottawatomie Creek, he resolutely put a pistol to the head of a proslavery settler and fired point-blank. A stern disciplinarian with his sons, he would urge his second wife to show restraint and kindness: "I want your face to shine even if my own should be dark and cloudy" (*JB* 48). At the end, in his death cell, Brown tried to avoid a last meeting with his wife, fearing it would be too emotionally devastating for her. When it was time for her to leave, it was Brown who momentarily "lost self-control" (*JB* 437). Abandoning his family for long stretches of time, first as part of his campaign to strike it big in a series of business ventures that inevitably ended in failure and later in the crusade for abolition, Brown nevertheless worried about their well-being and consistently gave the family's security high priority—even as his date with the gallows loomed nearer and nearer.

Neither a tarnished saint nor an altogether contemptible sinner, Warren's Brown is all too human. A Connecticut Yankee early transplanted to the western frontier, he is an American Adam, innocent by conviction if not in fact, adhering to a success ethic that confuses God and Mammon. He becomes a righteous warrior who never fails to keep his eye on the main chance. (Killing enemies of freedom in Kansas yields their horses.) Denied a career in the ministry by eye problems as a young man,[40] Brown nonetheless is a man who lives by words as much as through action. An inveterate student of the Bible, he felt compelled to generate texts of his own, and, in doing so, revealed himself and his sense of himself in ways that are not lost on his biographer. Indeed, the youthful Warren studies Brown's "texts" in a way that looks forward to Jack Burden's puzzling over the narrative of Cass Mastern in *All the King's Men* and the nameless historian narrator's presentation of the journal of Jeremiah Beaumont in *World Enough and Time*. Brown knew the magic inherent in the grand word—"Freedom," for example—and the word's potent capacity for shaping humankind's understanding of reality and thus reshaping reality itself. Unlike Emerson, portrayed by Warren (no doubt reductively) as a man who blithely accepted reality as purely rhetorical, Brown is a more dangerous idealist—one whose ideas and words are translated into the bloody language of violent action.

Brown's awareness of the power of the word extended itself to a grasp, quite modern in its application, of the importance of manipulating the media as a tool for directing public opinion. In Kansas, he had influenced newspaper accounts of the Osawatomie affair to turn paramilitary defeat into moral victory. After Harper's Ferry, he turned his trial, its conclusion self-evident from its very inception, into a strangely compelling kind of guerrilla theater. In the end, his words were to speak louder to many listeners than his undeniably treasonous actions, and he was to wrest from his final failure a measure of success that he had not foreseen. Thwarted as a man of letters, just as he had been in his courting of worldly riches, Brown finally, through an act of will (and willfulness), brought forth his most enduring and enigmatic text—his self-created Self.

One of Brown's actual texts, an autobiographical letter written to the young son of George Luther Stearns (one of the philanthropical New England contributors to Brown's anti-slavery crusade), is regarded by Warren as particularly revealing:

By the dirty oil lamps in hotel rooms, by his campfire, by the hot summer sunlight when he sat on the roadside, John Brown filled page after page with his tight, nearly illiterate handwriting. It was also the handwriting of an old man—cramped, irregular, painful—but it told what sort of a little boy "John" had been. "This story will be mainly a narration of follies and errors; which it is to be hoped *you* may *avoid;* but there is one thing connected with it, which will be calculated to encourage any young person to persevering effort; & that is the degree of success *in accomplishing his objects* which to a great extent marked the course of this boy throughout my entire acquaintance with him; nothwithstanding his moderate capacity; & still more moderate acquirements." The golden text of the document was underscored: "the degree of success *in accomplishing his objects.*" [*JB* 247-48]

On one level, the letter, Warren maintains, had as its purpose, like many Brown letters, the canny solicitation of financial support from the recipient's well-meaning parents. "But," Warren goes on to say, "there was another meaning to the letter," one "more profound, obscure, and necessary":

John Brown's head was full of a scheme whose magnitude and consequence no one but himself could guess. At last things were moving toward the fulfillment of that scheme; for the first time it seemed near and possible, and with this new possibility came the first dubieties and waverings. And so he wrote: "He followed up with *tenacity* whatever he set about so long as it answered the general purpose; & hence he rarely failed in some good degree to effect the things he undertook. This was so much the case that he *habitually expected to succeed* in his undertakings. With this feeling *should be coupled;* the consciousness that our plans are right in themselves," . . . but the rest sounds a little strange after the long history of so many failures. The letter was John Brown's letter to himself, written to wipe out just that history. What it said was this: "Those old failures are no matter, for I was *right*. And now, *now at this last, I am still right and I will not fail.*" [*JB* 248-49]

If this desire to erase the past and live in the glorious promise of the future—so unmistakably *American* an impulse—denies Brown the possibility of any real self-awareness, it does, however paradoxically, become the source of an undeniable strength of character, as Warren shows in his account of Brown's last days following the debacle at Harper's Ferry. Faced with the seeming collapse of his grandiose dreams, Brown may, as Warren contends, have momentarily sought refuge in a kind of vaguely defined fatalism, but, denied the opportunity of dying in battle, he stoutly maintained the ironic integrity of his self-image. He might lie shamelessly about his motives and intentions, but only as a means of nurturing his own higher "truth." The psychological quirks that always stood in the way of a genuine measure of self-knowledge conspired with circumstance to provide Brown with a triumph that overshadowed all failure:

Long ago in the few nondescript books of history which pieced out the ground rules of arithmetic in his education, John Brown had learned of a world outside of the frontier town, he had learned to dramatize himself, and he had learned the meaning of ambition. That tall, sedate, and dignified young man, with the imperious eye and the coarse hair brushed back on his unusually small head, had been very sure that he was right in all matters and very sure of his own worth. And so he beat his brothers, read his Bible, believed himself set apart from the vain and petty life around him, and, because he did not see how to escape that life, felt a steady, strong desire to die. He wanted desperately, as Milton Lusk [his brother-in-law] put it, to be head of the heap, and doubted, not his worth, but his opportunities. From the time when inflamed eyes stopped his ambition of becoming a minister . . . until the time he rode a murdered man's horse out of the Pottawatomie valley, every effort had ended in some unpredictable failure. Superb energy, honesty and fraud, chicanery, thrift, endurance, cruelty, conviction, murder, and prayer—they had all failed, only to leave him surer than before that he was right and that his plans were "right in themselves." [*JB* 428-29]

As a martyred prophet uttering grim warnings of fire and blood to come, Brown emerged triumphant. Only his death could redeem his life, so he adamantly refused to entertain a plea of insanity in his defense—to mitigate his actions in any way threatened the carefully formulated meaning he sought to attach to them. He could not be a heroic symbol if he were an irresponsible madman. Nor would Brown countenance the various quixotic schemes to rescue him from the gallows. Even had escape been somehow "miraculously accomplished," Brown knew that "he could not confront the consequences—a nine days' wonder and then an empty dwindling into old age with the consciousness of failure" (*JB* 427). As with Shakespeare's Thane of Cawdor, nothing in Brown's life so became him as his taking leave of it.

From an existential standpoint, Brown's act of self-immolation is less than authentically tragic since it is but a last manifestation of a lifelong self-delusion. Nevertheless, it is important to see how Warren accords this lying and murderous "martyr" a measure of personal integrity denied many of his co-conspirators in the North. If Brown is finally loathsome and monstrous, he is nevertheless more manly than the philanthropic idealists Gerrit Smith, Frank B. Sanborn, George Luther Stearns, and S.G. Howe, who to varying degrees repudiated Brown, their principles, and thus their very selves in an effort to escape their share of responsibility for the Harper's Ferry affair. They were determined not to pay the price of imprisonment or death for the luxury of practicing what they preached, though Warren, always evenhanded, notes that two other conspirators, Theodore Parker and Thomas Wentworth Higginson, remained unrepentant. These latter two may have earned the young southern author's reluctant respect, but respect does not necessarily entail approval. Indeed, the pages of *John Brown* are already informed by a characteristic "political" philosophy that Warren would develop and articulate with more clarity in his subsequent writings.

By indirection, Warren calls for a kind of social activism grounded in realpolitik but married to moral vision. John Brown is the negative image of the ideal citizen upon whom the ultimate success of America's democratic experiment de pends but Warren provides us with foils to Brown, though not all are viable. The legislative giants of the first half of the nineteenth century—Webster, Clay, and Calhoun—embody traits of character and principle that Warren clearly admires, but Warren shows that the crisis the nation faced over the slavery question had moved beyond their ineffectual efforts at compromise. Events were out of hand, though Warren seems to imply throughout *John Brown* that men, not fate or the zeitgeist, shape history; as Jack Burden comes to realize, "History is blind, but man is not."[41] Though Warren may see Colonel Lewis Washington, one of Brown's hostages at Harper's Ferry and a nephew of the first president, as a total gentleman of the old school, admirable for his uprightness and unimpeachable integrity, he nevertheless is quick to demonstrate how inadequate the Virginian planterly ideal was when it came to addressing an America in mortal crisis. Colonel Washington, taken hostage in the early stages of the raid on Harper's Ferry, does not even recognize the notorious name of John Brown, since, as he says, "'I have become so disgusted with Kansas and everything connected with it, that whenever I see a paper with "Kansas" at the head of it, I turn over and do not read'" (*JB* 355). It is precisely this same tendency to wash one's hands of the muck of irrationality and violence that is the undoing of the grandfather in Warren's story "Prime Leaf," written shortly after *John Brown*, and it will have tragic consequences for later characters like Captain Todd in *Night Rider* (1939).

What the times called for (and lacked in sufficient numbers, as the nation moved inexorably toward all-out civil war) was a breed of men who fought irrationality with a fully engaged reason and who sought to combat violence by taking legitimate means to sever its roots in injustice. Few such men existed, though for a time they *were* able to bring peace to bloody Kansas, where the Civil War had had its mini-rehearsal: "The men with a practical sense and a respect for the letter of the law . . . were the people who saved Kansas; they were the people who ran the Emigrant Aid Company or who broke the market for Missouri State bonds and made investors shout for an end to Missouri aggression in Kansas" (*JB* 229). These were citizens capable of taking drastic action without resorting to lawlessness or weapons, and it is vital to note that Warren includes among them a man of letters. The "man whose editorials broke the bonds," Warren reminds us, "was a poet, William Cullen Bryant by name." Implicit here, and throughout the "making" of *John Brown*, is Warren's sense of the role, the *active* role, the American writer is called upon to take in shaping the nation's destiny. "History is blind, but man is not"—and it is incumbent upon men and women of vision to strive to *see* through chaos and disorder to a viable restoration of civic and social order. The visionary company of poets is not exempt. *John Brown* itself figured forth a prophetic message about the perils of history and the self that, though largely ignored at the time, had an intense relevance to the American predicament of the next decade.

When the 1920s came to a close, Robert Penn Warren was already the author of a published book, and he had written a piece of fiction that would be included in the prestigious *American Caravan IV* (1931); still, he regarded himself primarily as a poet. Payson & Clarke, the publishers of *John Brown*, had agreed to bring out a collection of Warren's verse, but the firm was bankrupted in the Great Crash.[42] America faced its greatest threat to national survival since the war that had come in the wake of Harper's Ferry. His apprenticeship behind him, Warren would begin his mature career as a writer at a time when the nation seemed to teeter on the brink of utter collapse. Increasingly, Warren came to realize that history was no longer the romantic subject of moony poems, nor could it be addressed adequately with the rhetoric of *I'll Take My Stand*. History was here and now and admitted of no excuses. As Warren would say in 1974, "The Depression did a great deal to destroy the sense of historical fatalism, because you *had* to have action or die. There was a crisis there which *demanded* action. You could not accept history as finished, which is part of the Southern disease, and you had to reorder society, and this meant you had to reorder all sorts of relationships."[43] Warren's long journey toward America's first official laureateship began in earnest with the coming of the Great Depression, and it would wind through subsequent decades of war, national doubt, and civil strife before the prophet would find himself adequately honored in his own country.

3

Out of the Thirties

In 1930, having taken the B. Litt. at Oxford, Warren returned to the United States, and in that year the little magazine *This Quarter* carried his poem "Empire." Clearly born of the same impulse that had given rise to earlier verse like "Iron Beach" and "To a Face in the Crowd," it too seemed to presume that history—at least in the West—had come to an end. In a tone both epic and elegiac, Warren's speaker charts the westward course of empire from the days of the Phoenicians, Greeks, and Romans through the discovery and exploration of the New World by voyagers like Columbus and Hudson. As is frequently the case with Warren's verse, it is possible to see in "Empire" an implicit intertextual relationship with Whitman, and with "Passage to India" in particular. (The final line of the third stanza reads "passage to India, passage home.") But Warren, unlike Whitman, presents the circumnavigation of the globe and settling of the North American continent not as fulfillments of an age-old dream so much as stages in a journey toward futility, failure, and dissolution. With Columbus's vision redeemed through the "wonders" of modern technology, Whitman had argued that the human soul was freed at last to pursue a "passage to more than India."[1] Warren's protagonist, on the other hand, gazes out from the barren shores of spiritual oblivion. The heroic questers of the past were fully human, to be sure, at once "single-hearted and horizon-sick," but they possessed a purpose and certainty denied contemporary man, who in his ahistoricity is "bastard to memory," a "spotless white

/ new lamb, got of no sin, born to no wrath, / no home, no repentance."[2] To put it another way, the American, that "new man" whose arrival Crèvecoeur had lauded, was now no-man.

In its world-weariness, "Empire" is unmistakably a poem of the 1920s, a creditable enough study in a disillusioned sensibility more appropriate perhaps to writers of the Lost Generation. The America Warren had returned to faced far more compelling problems than a vacuousness bred of peace and prosperity. Indeed, half a century after his return from England, Warren was to describe his impressions upon repatriation in terms that even then testified to the violent shock he had received: "I came back to America to find New York a hellhole and people fist-fighting each other to take my suitcase for a dime."[3] The mingled aversion and compassion in Warren's description calls to mind a vivid scene from a novel by another southerner only five years Warren's senior. In *You Can't Go Home Again*, published posthumously, Thomas Wolfe described the plight of "uprooted, unwanted" victims of the Depression who "drifted across the land and gathered in the big cities when winter came, hungry, defeated, empty, hopeless, restless, . . . looking everywhere for work." For such men, a public rest room becomes a haven, and Wolfe, through the eyes of his autobiographical protagonist George Webber, recreates the nightmarish world of the dispossessed who occupy the "comfort station" immediately "in front of the New York City Hall": "George had never before witnessed anything to equal the indignity and sheer animal horror of the scene. There was even a kind of devil's comedy in the sight of all these filthy men squatting upon those open, doorless stools. Arguments and savage disputes and fights would sometimes break out among them over the possession of these stools, which all of them wanted more for rest than necessity. The sight was revolting, disgusting, enough to render a man forever speechless with very pity."[4] Shaken, George Webber emerges from this descent into the underworld to see Wall Street's shining "pinnacles of power" in stark relief against the night sky, and he feels a quickening of social conscience at the "blind injustice" of the times.

The direction Thomas Wolfe's social awareness would take

him turned out to be predictably idiosyncratic, but the intensity of his response to the bitter ironies posed by the Depression was anything but atypical.[5] For an increasing number of creative men and women, "the country's collective identity" seemed in the balance.[6] "The Depression," writes Robert S. McElvaine, "led many intellectuals into believing that some sort of social and ideological apocalypse was at hand. . . . The old world was collapsing and the chance was there to take a hand in molding a new one."[7] As we saw at the conclusion of the previous chapter, the Depression convinced Robert Penn Warren that history was not "finished," that the taking of responsible "action" was an unavoidable imperative. Yet Warren's response to that present crisis has not been properly understood. Critics intent upon placing his work under the rubric of the Southern Renascence have often neglected Warren's "politics" in favor of exploring his regional preoccupation with the past and adaptation of indigenous materials. Others, altogether too mindful of Warren's Agrarian credentials (he was always a maverick in the eyes of the more conservative members of that group), have tried to tar him with the brush of what Grant Webster has called "Tory Formalism."[8] The fact remains that Warren came into his maturity as a writer during the decade of the 1930s, and even his novels of the 1940s, *At Heaven's Gate* and *All the King's Men*, are belated expressions of the Depression era. The literature of the 1930s was of necessity politicized; the realm of letters, like the bloody Harlan County in Warren's native Kentucky, was a battleground where there were "no neutrals"—at least from the perspective of those radical leftist writers who managed to frame the terms of the ongoing debate over the artist's obligations to society. If we would understand the genuinely prophetic aspects of Warren's place in our national literature, we must reinterpret his Depression years, spent variously as poet, critic, editor, and fictionist, in the light of the literary politics raging around him.

In this regard, the year 1935 is crucial. The New Deal, through fits and starts, was at least under way. The National Recovery Administration might be declared unconstitutional, but Social Security and the WPA were put in place, and a growing hope had begun to leaven the despair that had deepened in the nadir years 1932-33. Whatever guarded optimism might be in the air, Warren obviously had personal and professional reasons of his own for encouragement in 1935. At last a volume of his selected poems was published, and his relatively enviable position as a faculty member at Louisiana State University now offered him an unanticipated opportunity to make a decided difference in the realms of letters and informed public opinion. With Charles W. Pipkin and Cleanth Brooks, Warren was to edit a new quarterly, the *Southern Review*.[9]

As fate (or the "forces of history") would have it, 1935 was also the year in which the anthology *Proletarian Literature in the United States*, edited by Granville Hicks, Michael Gold, and others, appeared. Though it contained nearly four hundred pages, it purported to be much less inclusive than its editors would have ideally desired. Necessity, it seems, had dictated that it be "restricted to its present size, in order to make possible the publication of a low-priced volume within the reach of workers and students."[10] The book's function as agitprop unabashedly bearing the imprimatur of the Communist party was never in question. For that very reason, it provides us with a convenient leftist touchstone for testing Warren's own literary/political values.

While conceding that Marxist orthodoxy in and of itself could not guarantee the artistic success of a poem or short story, the editors of *Proletarian Literature* nonetheless maintained that every work of literature inevitably represented the interests of a given social class and thus, willy-nilly, functioned as a revolutionary or reactionary weapon in the class struggle made manifest by the seeming collapse of capitalism. The appeal to universal human experience in literature and, even worse, the self-indulgence of the doctrine of art for art's sake, were not simply harmless vestiges of a discredited bourgeois mindset; they were pernicious, unconsciously undermining revolutionary change and bolstering the cause of reaction, if not indirectly giving aid and comfort to the Fascists.[11] By contrast, a "proletarian" poem, even when cast in a decadent form like that of the sonnet, might strike a blow for justice. Witness Alfred Kreymborg's "American Jeremiad":

It's pretty hard to sing of moonlight now,
Of benches in the park and lovers' lanes.
I'd like to if I could, but here somehow
Are shadows, beggars, shadows, and the rain's
A dripping, soppy, clammy winding-sheet
Indifferent to the tragedies of men,
Indifferent as the many passing feet
That make the beggars rise and drop again.

What shall a lover sing when half the land
Is driven cold and lives on dank despair?
As long as inhumanity's in the hand
That runs the race and whips the poor apart,
Lovers must all embrace a bloody air
And strangle men who starve the human heart.[12]

The position of Hicks, Gold, and Joseph Freeman, is, of
course, an extreme one, but it provided, in a somewhat qualified form, a set of assumptions for Left-leaning critics like
Robert Lann, who reviewed Warren's *Thirty-Six Poems* (along
with William Carlos Williams's *An Early Martyr*) for the *New
Republic*. Asserting that Warren "succeeds far oftener than he
fails, because there is in most of his poems a hard fidelity to
experience," Lann felt obligated to end his review with an
expression of regret that the verse of Warren and Williams
"does not seem to be part of the continuing line of social
development."[13] In short, the poems in Warren's first collection, for all their skill and power, evade the pressing issues of
the time. We need not accept Lann's underlying assumptions
about the social responsibility of the artist in order to recognize that the fundamental theses informing *Thirty-Six Poems*
are ontological rather than economic. Still, it would be a
serious mistake to suppose that Warren's poetry is evasive and
insular, a product of his privileged academic status and quite
divorced from the political drama acted out daily in the streets
and on the strike-lines. Nor will it do to suggest that whatever
ideological slant the poems do reveal is identifiably "Agrarian"—at least in any meaningful sense of the term. Warren's
poems of the 1930s are not the work of a man who seeks to
avoid commitment so much as they are expressions of his
unwillingness to commit himself utterly and prematurely to

any rigid ideology. In writing *John Brown,* Warren had learned that even the noblest ideals may seduce the idealist into abandoning his better self.[14] With the exception of poems like "To a Face in the Crowd,"[15] poems of the previous decade, Warren's first book of selected verse may even—up to a point—be regarded profitably as a kind of Depression document.

The Depression manifests itself in some startling ways. In "The Return: An Elegy," a meditative lyric so intense as to seem autobiographical to some readers,[16] the dominant mood is shockingly interrupted by a macabre instance of panhandling:

> give me the nickels off your eyes
> from your hand the violets
> let me bless your obsequies
> if you possessed conveniently enough three eyes
> then I could buy a pack of cigarettes.[17]

By the same token, the "drought-bit ground" that "deflects the plow" ("Resolution") and "the dusty road" ("Aged Man Surveys the Past Time") evoke contemporary images of the Dustbowl as much as they echo the imagery of *The Waste Land.* These are poems written in "the time of toads' engendering" ("Letter to a Friend"):

> Empires collide with a bang
> That shakes the pictures where they hang
> And democracy shows signs of dry rot
> And Dives has and Lazarus not
> And the time is out of joint.
>
> [*TSP* 38]

So, appropriately enough, speaks the Hamlet-like persona in "Letter from a Coward to a Hero," a poem that implies that a failure of nerve may pose as circumspection even as heroic commitment to revolution may conceal the death wish. (Significantly, the hero here has *not yet* had occasion "to pawn" his courage.) The dialectic of "confrontation and retreat" that John Burt identifies as characteristic of Warren's "poetic method,"[18] is fully in effect in *Thirty-Six Poems.* If, like his Agrarian brethren, Warren is unwilling to sacrifice the claims of the individuated and independent self in order to embrace a collectivist prescription for the future, simultaneously he rejects the aims of sentimental reactionaries who pursue a "backward calendar" toward a Golden Age ruled by "sages" and enlightened monarchs ("Toward Rationality"). The partisans of tomorrow and the champions of yesterday alike rush after a phantom quarry, like the invisible hunters in the poem "Eidolon." Meanwhile, "the old zeal" (the Jeffersonian dream?) is "Yet unfulfilled, unratified, unlaced"—"our courage needs, perhaps, new definition" ("Ransom").

Better than any other single poem in the collection, "History" spells out the troubled and ambivalent state of Warren's American vision during this period. An obvious extension of the theme of empire and national origins that had preoccupied him in several earlier poems, "History" provides a synoptic account of American experience in terms of the pervasive myth of the New World as a new Canaan, a myth Warren would counter more emphatically nearly two decades later in *Brother to Dragons*. After a long trial of hunger, privation, and aimless wandering in a hostile wilderness, the chosen people of Warren's poem enjoy a glimpse of the promised land:

> It is a land of corn and kine,
> of milk
> And wine,
> And beds that are as silk:
> The gentle thigh,
> The unlit night-lamp nigh.
> This much was prophesied:
> We shall possess,
> And abide
> —Nothing less.
> We may not be denied.
> The inhabitant shall flee as the fox;
> His foot shall be among the rocks.
> [*TSP* 30-31]

The native population expelled, the conquerors' "seed shall prosper" in the "new land," and, relieved of hardship, "Our sons shall cultivate / Peculiar crimes, / Having not love, nor hate, / Nor memory" (*TSP* 31). These lines recall the Agrarians' indictment of the fruits of industrial capitalism in the days before the Great Crash, but Warren also submits that it is equally possible to become an impotent slave to nostalgia and memory:

> . . . some
> Of all most weary,
> Most defective of desire,
> Shall grope toward time's cold womb;
> In dim pools peer
> To see, of some grandsire,
> The long and toothèd jawbone greening there.
>
> [*TSP* 32]

In "Ode to the Confederate Dead," Tate had dutifully noted the dangers of establishing the "ravenous grave" in the "house" of the living,[19] and Warren shares such fears. Nevertheless, his race of conquerors, assured that destiny, if not God, is on their side, that they are merely "doom's apparitor[s]," revel in a radical innocence in which "The act / Alone is pure" and the compulsions of history excuse all things.

There is a typical Warrenesque synchronicity at work in "History," an implicit sense of the way in which the mythic past reflects the realities of the present. If the descendants of the conquerors are to know an era of prosperity and ease that breeds decadence, there will also come a time when a generation as yet unborn and unnamed will "know dearth / And flame." In 1935, that time had indeed come, and a new set of would-be masters surveyed the future's Promised Land, armed with a theoretical apologetics for violence. The most blatant proponents of such an apologetics might be Marxist in their orientation and nurture an internationalist perspective in their approach to the ills of the Depression, but Warren's poem serves to demonstrate how receptive the American collective imagination was to just such millennial visions.

Arthur M. Schlesinger, Jr., has shown how adherents of American "destiny" have claimed for themselves a heady brand of "messianism" that in effect provides them with a moral carte blanche.[20] To translate such convictions into the secular terminology of class struggle was not as difficult as it might seem at first glance, which may do much to explain the relative ease with which American intellectuals of privileged background and unquestionable perspicuity, like Edmund Wilson and (for a longer time) Malcolm Cowley, identified their interests with that of a sentimentalized proletariat.[21] Warren, on the other hand, retained a stubborn skepticism toward millennialism in every form. Like William James, he might be said to represent a native strain of what Schlesinger calls American "realism."[22] History for Warren was not a predestined unfolding of events in which amoral means might be counted upon to contribute to ultimately just ends,[23] it remained subject to human experiment, with all the contingency of human fallibility called into play. The final triumph of justice was forever problematic.

While such an awareness is not unique with Warren, it permeates his work with such intensity as to give rise to what Burt has termed Warren's characteristically "elegiac politics"—though Burt seems to overestimate the degree to which Warren's moral circumspection and distrust of absolutes tend to inhibit action.[24] The author of *Thirty-Six Poems*, at least from his own perspective, *was* actively engaged in social issues. The fact that he gladly contributed to the Agrarian/ Distributist symposium *Who Owns America?* speaks for itself—even if Warren's piece in that volume is typically balanced and non-doctrinaire—for *Who Owns America?* is a radical response to the crisis of capitalism brought on by the Depression, an incisive critique framed from a traditionalist angle of vision. Behind it stands a more definite, if broadly defined, political agenda than one finds in the far more nebulous *I'll Take My Stand*, and, for our purposes, Warren's contribution, "Literature as a Symptom," furnishes important insight into his views on the artist's proper relationship to society.

Warren insists in "Literature as a Symptom" that there has never been a period in history when "the novelist or poet" has been "relieved of the responsibility of inspecting the aims of the society" of which he or she is a part.[25] Ideally, the writer engages in literary activity "as a part, and perhaps the most

significant part, of his role as a citizen and a human being."
However, Warren also insists upon a revealing caveat: even a
writer like Milton, who "was directly involved in a revolutionary movement" (*WOA* 268), must never cease "functioning *as*
artist" (*WOA* 269) if he hopes to produce "a genuine creation"
(*WOA* 267). Implicit here is Warren's conviction that a vital
work of literature, like the world it embodies, cannot be comfortably circumscribed by a given party line, whether proletarian or "regionalist." Human beings and the events they
shape and are shaped by are simply too complex and self-
contradictory to admit to a distorting reductionism.

Warren's politics parallel his poetics, for history has its
paradoxes and ironies as surely as a sonnet by Donne or a play
by Shakespeare. Policies, if they are to do justice to those they
effect, must constantly be refined through experiment and
testing. The way of abstraction is the way toward self-defeat.
Simple answers can never satisfy humankind's yearning for
philosophical understanding, and facile solutions to questions
of social injustice never suffice for long. Warren shared with
the Marxists a dialectical mode of thought, but his dialectic
resists bipolarization. It is driven by socio-economic tensions
up to a point, but it incorporates psychological and spiritual
divisions at every stage of the struggle. By the mid-1930s,
Warren had hit upon his own version of "politics as process,"
though it would be wrong to downplay the influence Ransom
and Tate's respective theories on poetic "irony" and "tension"
may have had on its formulation.[26]

Reviewing Edna St. Vincent Millay's *Wine from These Grapes*
for the *Southwest Review* in 1935, Cleanth Brooks faulted the
poet for her lack of "maturity" in handling social questions:
"Miss Millay's implied faith in palliatives somewhat vitiates
the quality of her irony." "Irony," Brooks continued, "is in one
sense the poet's coming to terms with those elements of experience which conflict with what he [sic] desires or approves—
with the ugly, the negative, and the evil. The greatest poetry
always does come to terms with them. They are synthesized in
the total vision, which is total only because it is able to include

them."[27] This insistence upon an inclusive "total vision" became a central tenet of the New Criticism Brooks and Warren were soon to introduce into the college classroom through a series of textbooks that would revolutionize the teaching of literature to an entire generation, and it should be pointed out that a similar commitment to "total vision," a vision open to antitheses, was the primary strength of the *Southern Review* during the Brooks and Warren years. Initially, the political scientist Charles W. Pipkin might be the designated editor (which accounts in part for the attention to current affairs from the beginning), but managing editors Brooks and Warren shouldered their full share of responsibility for shaping the *Review* from the outset. Pipkin was oriented more toward New South and "progressive" views than his junior colleagues, which clearly served to promote in and of itself a pluralistic balance in the *Review*'s pages, but even after Pipkin's growing disengagement Brooks and Warren successfully maintained a quarterly that sought to establish literary and intellectual vitality—rather than ideological orthodoxy—as its determining criterion.[28]

A partial survey of the first issue of the *Southern Review* is instructive. The lead essay was by Tate's recent ally Herbert Agar, whose "Culture versus Colonialism in America" was a rousing call for national self-examination and a repudiation of those "defeatists" who claimed that the future for America must be either Fascist or Communist: "Our hope lies in the fact that we once had a political tradition which could give an answer in terms of freedom to the false fascist-or-communist dilemma. We have weakened that tradition shamefully, by taking its name in vain. We have betrayed it item by item while assuring each other that we were merely adapting it to modern progress. It will not be easily revived today. Yet there is our job. All over the United States men are waking to that knowledge at last."[29] Agar's call for Jeffersonian renewal was followed by a discussion of literary "techniques" by Ford Madox Ford, Katherine Anne Porter's classic story "The Circus," and a pointed analysis of the practical problems attendant upon Agrarianism by an old nemesis of the movement, Rupert B.

Vance. R.K. Gooch wrote on French radicalism, and a protest poem of sorts by Lincoln Fitzell appeared opposite Donald Davidson's ironic musings on the Nashville Parthenon. Poets of the stature of Wallace Stevens and R.P. Blackmur graced this inaugural issue, but so did a relative newcomer, Randall Jarrell. The inclusion of a story by Caroline Gordon came as no surprise, but an omnibus poetry review by the decidedly leftist critic Kenneth Burke must have given pause to readers who assumed that the *Southern Review* was to be a closed forum for traditionalists. Brooks and Warren were determined to sponsor new talent, especially from the South, even as they launched a quarterly of international distinction,[30] a fact readily borne out in this issue, which featured portions of a novel by the ill-fated Oklahoman Edward Donahoe as well as an essay by Aldous Huxley.

The second issue of the *Review* was like unto the first. There was Ransom's "The Tense of Poetry" and an essay, "The Modern State: Karl Marx and Mr. Laski," by former Fugitive William Yandell Elliott but also a critique of the New Deal by Norman Thomas, who would in time become the grand old man of American socialism. In the pro-union "Labor and Race Prejudice," George Sinclair Mitchell developed an idea Warren had anticipated in "The Briar Patch" ("It costs working people money to be prejudiced"),[31] and Brooks and Warren no doubt took comfort from a statement by Herbert Read that confirmed their own aesthetics and, by extension, vindicated the editorial policies they and Pipkin were pursuing. "The poet," wrote Read, ". . . cannot, without renouncing his essential function, come to rest in the bleak conventicles of a political party. It is not his pride that keeps him outside; it is really his humility, his devotion to the complex wholeness of humanity."[32]

Allen Tate, for all his cultivation of complexity in poetry and scorn for the abstractive tendencies of the modern mind, was not so sure that a critical quarterly should present a broad range of viewpoints with apparent equanimity, and in the third issue of the *Southern Review* he argued for the necessity of a principled "dogmatism." Though Tate was to see the shortcomings of a specifically *southern* conservatism to a degree Davidson and Lytle never did, he felt himself and his position so embattled in the 1930s that he was loath to give those outside the fold a platform for broadcasting error.[33] Tate's "The Function of the Critical Quarterly" ended on a note that carried with it an admonition. The editor "owes his first duty to his critical principles, his sense of the moral and intellectual order upon which society ought to rest," Tate argued: "At a time when action has become singularly devoid of intelligence, there could not be a 'cause' more disinterested. The way to give the public what it resentfully needs is to discredit the inferior ideas of the age by exposing them to the superior ideas."[34] Brooks and Warren might have countered that such was precisely their intention in juxtaposing divergent points of view, but it is clear from a letter of November 30, 1935, to Warren that Tate was not to be persuaded by that kind of argument. In his letter, Tate deplored the lack of a proper ideological focus in the fledgling *Review*, though an appended note suggests that the force of his criticism was aimed at providing Warren with ammunition to use for his own purposes against Pipkin.[35]

Though they may have differed with Tate—and indeed with each other—on specifics, Brooks and Warren clearly identified their "cause" with his. Nevertheless, they refused to purge the *Southern Review* of ideological impurities even as they gradually gained full control. They would welcome Lytle on Calhoun but also publish Sidney Hook on Trotsky. Not only the relatively safe John Dewey, but James T. Farrell, Max Eastman, Philip Rahv, and Mary McCarthy were among the contributors from the Left. In another context, Brooks and Warren once acknowledged that "the socio-economico-pathologico-Marxist critical method" had on occasion "led, though not inevitably, to some trenchant, instructive, provocative, and even plausible, remarks."[36] They had in mind, among others, Edmund Wilson and Malcolm Cowley, but included Granville Hicks, one of the editors of *Proletarian Literature*, in their backhanded praise. Even so, given the volatile and often bitter intensity of literary politics in the 1930s, it is worthy of note that Brooks and Warren eventually published in the *Southern Review* a short story by the Communist fellow traveler Grace Lumpkin, who had sought to discredit their magazine shortly after its inception by associating it with Seward Collins's avowedly Fascist *American Review.*[37]

Brooks and Warren indeed contributed to Collins's short-lived journal before its editor's politics became patently embarrassing,[38] as did Agar, Tate, and others of the *Who Owns America?* group, but their views appeared in company with those of a wide-ranging set of traditionalists that included the humanist Paul Elmer More, British Catholics like G.K. Chesterton, Hilaire Belloc, and Father M.C. D'Arcy, and independent-minded American critics like Mark Van Doren and Austin Warren. An avowed "royalist" like Eliot and the pro-Fascist Wyndham Lewis were contributors (one wonders why Pound was not), but so was that irascible democrat Yvor Winters. In the pages of the *American Review,* as elsewhere, Brooks and Warren spoke for themselves, as would Warren somewhat later in placing his work with the *Partisan Review,* which had begun as an organ of the John Reed Club before gaining its autonomy under the inspired editorship of Philip Rahv and William Phillips—who nevertheless firmly retained the Marxist slant of the quarterly.[39] As contributors to periodicals, Brooks and Warren followed the same philosophy that governed their editorial procedures. They were eager to be part of the passionate political/cultural dialogue of the 1930s, but no idea, even one of their own, was too sacred to be subject to testing.

Though we remember the *Southern Review* today almost exclusively in terms of the impact it made on modern literature, we ought not to forget that in issue after issue it fostered an ongoing dialogue on questions involving the New Deal, the failure of the League of Nations, the relative virtues of an Open Door Policy, trade unionism, and the future of American neutrality in the face of increasingly ominous events in Europe and Asia. When the Second World War came, the *Review* itself would be an indirect casualty,[40] and an editorial announcing its discontinuation is worth quoting at length for the light it sheds on the editors' intentions from the start:

The Southern Review has never announced an "editorial policy," yet it is the hope of the editors that readers from this vantage point, looking back over the last seven years, will be able to discern a continuity of critical discussion, which, if it cannot be crystallized around a "policy," has none the less given to the magazine a character and a point of view. Indeed, the principal regret of the editors at terminating the career of the magazine lies in their conviction that in the difficult days ahead most of the issues and most of the problems which the magazine has undertaken to discuss will take on a heightened urgency and importance. The present impelling necessity for national unity, the pressure on the writer to contribute directly toward that national unity, the preoccupation at this time with means rather than ends, may succeed in obscuring or over-riding certain issues rather than in solving them. But the basic issues, though they may be over-ridden or obscured, remain issues still.

It is for these reasons that the editors, in releasing this last number of the magazine, feel that, in intention at least, the *Review* has made a contribution toward the examination of issues which, far from now being out of date, are living, vital, crucial. Indeed, it is the editors' conviction that an examination of them has involved an examination of some of the important problems to be solved in the building of our postwar civilization.[41]

The key terms in this understated, tentative, but all-the-more-striking, document are "discussion" and "examination," terms that underscore a sense that the truth—about the nature of literature, about the establishment of a just and workable social order, and about ourselves—can only be approached through an experiential process of point/counterpoint. It would be altogether wrong to suggest in any way that Brooks and Warren were nascent relativists. Their own reviews and essays of the 1930s demonstrate how aggressively they argued for and applied what Tate would call their principles and what somewhat less sympathetic readers might, quite understandably, identify as their biases. Brooks's *Modern Poetry and the Tradition* (1939), we ought to recall, was in many ways a polemical book, and Warren certainly never minced words in pointing out where he felt T.S. Stribling and Thomas Wolfe had gone wrong. Nevertheless, the common principles—or biases—they reasoned from were both the product of a dialectical process and a mechanism for furthering it. Warren engaged himself in the process at every level, recognizing full well that it was unlikely to provide ready panaceas, however desirable.

In terms of what Herbert Read had to say about a genuine poet's "humility" in the face of "the complex wholeness of humanity," it seems fair to argue that virtually all aspects of Warren's career in the years leading up to the Second World War reveal the presence of an abiding, though wholly secularized, *humilitas*. Because he was always aware of the mote in his own eye and never lost sight of his own capacity for arrogance and error, Warren managed to elude what Read called the "bleak conventicles" of blind partisanship. There would be no need for him, like Ransom, to dissociate himself formally from the bright but impractical dream of Agrarianism. More important, Warren's actions during the Depression years would never give him occasion to feel the intense remorse so many of his politically committed counterparts on the Left experienced when their loyalty was betrayed by Stalin's purges and nonaggression pact with Hitler. Chief among these was Warren's friend at the *New Republic*, Malcolm Cowley, whose own ideological odyssey, interestingly enough, parallels the progress from innocence through initiation that the Warren protagonist often undergoes.[42] Warren's politics might be "elegiac," but they were ultimately the politics of prudence, not unlike those of Franklin Roosevelt, whom he openly admired. At a time when violent rhetoric connived at real bloodshed, discretion—which is hardly apathy—may indeed have been the better part of valor.

In 1939, reviewing Lionel Trilling's book on Matthew Arnold for the *Kenyon Review*, Warren wrote: "Arnold does not give us solutions. But he gave us his poems, for which we are in his debt."[43] Allowing for a shift in context, Warren's remark might be applied with equal justice to his own creative output in the 1930s and early 1940s. As with the best of Arnold's verse, Warren's poetry following the publication of *Thirty-Six Poems*, collected in *Eleven Poems on the Same Theme* (1942), is a response to an unstable and shifting culture in crisis, a dramatization of inner conflicts that mirror macrocosmic tensions and turmoil. Marked by a heightened technical sophistication, a denser, more "metaphysical" texture, these poems catalogue the maimed Self's doomed attempts to flee from threats that are at once psychic and societal. They chronicle the efforts of their unnamed, and therefore representative, protagonist to deny his personal past and abandon as well the accompanying burdens of history. Whether the flight is toward an indeterminate future of limitless possibility or an erotic Eden of orgasmic oblivion matters little. Short of death, there is no exit from the human condition.

Significantly, for the secluded lovers in "Bearded Oaks," it is worldly "violence" that lends the "present stillness all its power."[44] The nature of that violence is made more specific in "Love's Parable," where the speaker tells his mistress, "we have seen the fungus eyes / Of misery spore in the night":

> And marked how ripe injustice flows,
> How ulcerous, how acid, then
> How proud flesh on the sounder grows
> Till rot engross the estate of men;
> [EP (20)][45]

Even more topical is the final poem of the collection, "Terror," which draws upon Warren's firsthand observation of Fascist Italy gearing up for war and alludes in no uncertain terms to the lethal idealism of the Abraham Lincoln Brigade in Spain, an idealism misspent in light of the Soviet assault upon Finland. An eager willingness to kill and die for a cause—be it on the Right or the Left—is, Warren shows, often merely another effort to abdicate the imperatives of selfhood. It was at bottom a "passionate emptiness and tidal / Lust" that brought many Americans to the "debris of Madrid" where they spent a "fierce idyll" before moving on to the arctic "North" where now "They fight old friends, for their obsession knows / Only the immaculate itch, not human foes" (EP 23). Even so, as Warren makes clear in the final stanza of "Terror," the times preclude an insular separate peace born of self-sustained indifference. The unengaged noncombatant who seeks to remain "guiltless" by turning a deaf ear to the world's rage and a blind eye to the state terrorism of dictatorial regimes is an object of special scorn.[46]

In recent years, the poetry of Warren's early maturity has tended to be overlooked in favor of the more readily accessible verse of his late period,[47] but it continues to repay careful study, particularly when read against the backdrop of the cataclysmic era in which it was written, for these poems realize in practice the premises of Warren's evolving aesthetic, an aesthetic that obviously corresponds to a tough-minded and pragmatic politics. They are of their time but never circumscribed by it. One reviewer of *Eleven Poems* summed up the matter with admirable succinctness: "Warren speaks from a rich memory of his craft and an imagination able to sever itself from the clutch of time and circumstance. This freedom is not laxity: the tone and rhythm are strict, austere, and penetrating as the spirit. Throughout we hear the refrain of apprehension, potential guilt, the social break-up into uneasy atoms—but distilled, often muted, perceptible through a harmonious personal music."[48]

Virtually all readers of Warren's work have identified the pedal point of his characteristic music as a pervasive sense of Original Sin (the title of one of the best known of *Eleven Poems*). Social activists typically despise the concept, arguing that a theory that begins with the assumption that humanity must inevitably fall short of perfection compromises our faith in meaningful progress and reinforces the arguments of reactionaries.[49] Warren's writing demonstrates that such need not be the case, as does that of another Southerner, who wrote during the Depression:

I am a Communist by sympathy and conviction. But it does not appear (just for one thing) that Communists have recognized . . . that the persistence of what once was insufficiently described as Pride, a mortal sin, can quite as coldly and inevitably damage and wreck the human race as the most total power of 'Greed' ever could: and that socially anyhow, the most dangerous form of pride is neither arrogance nor humility, but its mild, common denominator form, complacency. . . .

Certainly we don't know now, and never will, all of even the human truth. But we may as well admit we know a few things, and take full advantage of them. It is probably never really wise, or even necessary, or anything better than harmful, to educate a human being toward a good end by telling him lies.[50]

The author of these sentiments, which sound much like the hard-earned wisdom of a Warren antihero, is none other than James Agee, whose *Let Us Now Praise Famous Men* (1941)—a book that begins by quoting the *Communist Manifesto* and for all practical purposes ends with recitation of the Lord's Prayer—is one of the most celebrated American artifacts to survive the Great Depression. Incorporating photographs by Walker Evans that have since been designated American icons in their own right, *Let Us Now Praise Famous Men* had its genesis in the Depression era's compulsion to *document* social injustice.[51] But it did not stop there. The Alabama tenant farmers and their families whose lives Agee subjected to such fierce and loving scrutiny are unarguably victims of an oppressive economic system, yet they cannot be reduced to individual case histories. They "crop on shares," but at the same time share a common human predicament with the author and his privileged reader. Richard Wright, in working through *Native Son* (1940), discovered much the same thing about his black "victim" Bigger Thomas. Warren, unresponsive to the appeal of Marxism from the outset but always sensitive to the conditions that gave rise to protest literature,[52] likewise had occasion to document the plight of those at the bottom of the class and caste structure in his Depression fiction. Like the best of the proletarian writers, he delineated the pathos of poverty, exploitation, and neglect with uncompromising relentlessness at times, while never denying the downtrodden and dispossessed their full share—for good or ill—in the inheritance of Adam. This accounts in large measure for much of the vestigial power of Warren short stories like "Christmas Gift" (1936) and "Her Own People" (1935), stories that effectively set the conventions of standard protest fiction on end without in any way implying an apologetics for the status quo.

"Christmas Gift" is a stark slice of life featuring the ten-year-old son of an impoverished cropper, Milt Alley (alluded to at length in a later story, the often-anthologized "Blackberry Winter"). The boy is sent to fetch a country doctor to tend his half-sister, in labor with an illegitimate child. Warren's descriptions of the frigid weather, the bleak interior of the settlement store where the boy asks directions (and meets with ridicule as well as kindness), and the genteel tawdriness of the physician's parlor bear all the naturalistic detail and evocative force commonly associated with social realism. The boy is pitiable, and his plight occupies stage center, but Warren has taken pains to place the central action of the story in a wider context of human suffering that economic reform alone cannot alleviate. There is, for instance, the kidney disease of John Graber's wife and Graber's own drunkenness. Is Graber's drinking brought on by the stress of his wife's impending death? Or is it an ongoing part of the difficult life he has led her? The reader cannot be sure, and Warren's ambiguity here is functional. What matters is that Graber, whatever the reason, is of no help to the dying woman, though the doctor, who is in a position to know the details of the matter, refrains from judgment. The doctor's nonjudgmental approach to life is, along with a weary but unfailing sense of duty, his defining trait of character, as might be expected of one who practices his profession under the most frustrating of conditions. But there may be an explanation for his attitude even closer to home. His wife's actions betray symptoms of neurasthenia. Is her state an ironic consequence of her husband's healing art?

The world of "Christmas Gift" is a world where poverty is the norm; even the doctor and his wife are far removed from affluence. But it is also a world in which common acquaintance with misery breeds a respect for human dignity, and this respect is due even the son of a despised cropper (despised not for his destitution, it must be stressed). Dignity, however, demands outward signs of self-respect. When the doctor's wife reminds the boy that he should take off his hat in the house, she has no intention of humiliating him, and he takes no offense. Throughout, he is self-conscious and ashamed of his begrimed appearance; it is all too apparent to him and everyone else. But the man who cruelly teases him in the general store risks a beating from one of his fellows. There is no romanticizing of southern virtues here, though virtues as well as vices are depicted in a spare, wholly objective manner. The time of the story is indefinite, and indeed may be pre-Depression (the physician is literally a horse-and-buggy doctor), but the reader who first encountered it when it was published in 1937 would not have missed its particular relevance. Warren raises the politically-charged question of tenantry in no uncertain terms:

"What's your pappy doing now?" the doctor asked.
"My pappy's croppin' on a place for Mr. Porsum, but hit ain't no good."

. . . .

"We be leaving this year. We ain't gonna have no truck no more with Mr. Porsum, that ole son of a bitch. He ain't done nuthin' like he said. He ain't—"
"That's what your pappy says," the man said.
"My pappy says he's a goddam sheep-snitchin' son-a-bitch."
The man stared through the isinglass pane, his sharp nose and chin sticking out in front, his head wobbling with the motion of the buggy. Then he opened his mouth: "I reckon Jim Porsum's got something to say on his side." [53]

The doctor's response is altogether in keeping with his habitual unwillingness to pass judgments and assign blame. Furthermore, he clearly knows things about Milt Alley to which the reader is not privy. Still, a Marxist critic might argue that the doctor is predictably defending the interests of his "class," though the term seems oddly out of place in the society depicted here. Even admitting a measure of validity in such an interpretation, one should hasten to assert that the doctor is defending a person, Jim Porsum, not a long-standing structure of agricultural peonage, and in no way can he be said to speak for the author himself. Warren is content to allow character and situation to do the talking on their own terms. His truly *documentary* approach relies upon dramatic presentation rather than intrusive discourse and heavy-handed oversimplification to make its point.

"Christmas Gift" ends with a moment of significant interaction between the boy and the doctor that invites, but somehow eludes, sentimental treatment. At a more superficial level, it might easily have served as the climactic scene in a Frank Capra film. The boy offers the man half a stick of the hard candy he was given earlier in the store, and the doctor accepts it in a matter-of-fact way.[54] Norman Rockwell would have found this image quite congenial, but Warren's handling of it is more in keeping with the effect derived from the photographs Dorothea Lange, Arthur Rothstein, and others made under the auspices of the Farm Security Administration, some of the best of which were, like Warren's story, studiedly artful constructions.[55] It would be difficult to find much in the way of affirmation in this ending. At best, it might be said that the story concludes on a note of stoic solidarity. Warren denies the reader the mitigating comfort of ideology.

The same is true of "Her Own People," which is of particular importance by virtue of the way it portrays interracial relationships and the psychological wounds racism gives rise to, concerns that would occupy much of Warren's attention in the 1950s and 1960s. In recounting the frustrations a young white couple experience when their black cook, Viola, abandons them, Warren implies a wry commentary on the degree to which the dominant race is dependent upon the subordinate, a theme black Americans have understandably relished. But comic exasperation is soon replaced by growing hopelessness as the young black woman's debilitating mental illness becomes a fact not to be ignored, a fact that neither her white employees nor the older black couple with whom she lives can dispel. Rather boldly, Warren deals here with a subject that remains touchy in our own time—black self-loathing.

Abstracted from the particularized framework of Warren's narrative, Viola can be seen to belong to a class of stock characters that recur frequently in American fiction. She is a variation on the tragic mulatto type. The product of generations of white sexual transgressions of the color-line, she is more Caucasian than black, yet a social fiction with no basis in biological reality excludes her from the white world whose materialism and consumerism she nonetheless pitifully mimics. Viola has appropriated the racial mythology of her time and

place and internalized it to such an extent that she regards all
blacks as inherently "dirty"—a notion Warren goes to some
length to demolish in the story. Viola's anguish is clearly socially induced. She is a by-product of the irrational and dehumanizing system of segregation, but to admit that fact in no
way offers a solution to her quandary. Her anguish has moved
beyond neurosis, already present in her childhood, to utter
collapse. Her condition in turn torments those around her, irrespec-
tive of color. In "Her Own People," as in "Christmas Gift,"
Warren permits the unadorned "facts" of his fiction to speak a
direct, unmediated language of their own, and the resulting
indictment of social evils is more immediate and damaging
than any overt editorializing could make it. Warren learned
from reading T.S. Stribling that a naturalistic approach to
southern racial mores was "necessarily incomplete,"[56] just as
he learned from Faulkner how it was possible to see in region-
ally specific materials the germ of a genuinely tragic vision.
Thus "Her Own People" remains compelling reading today,
whereas a story like Erskine Caldwell's "Daughter," more representative of the social realism of the 1930s (and included in
Proletarian Literature in the United States), has taken on the
status of a rather quaint period piece. Warren understood
clearly enough the social dynamics of human suffering, but he
never allowed himself to ignore its fundamentally existential
dimension. For Warren, political theory always remained a
branch of philosophical inquiry, not an adequate substitute for
it.

Many American writers of the 1930s underwent a political
conversion experience akin in terms of its sudden violence to
being born again.[57] Warren never did, or at least never admitted to it. But his career is marked by certain epiphanic moments nonetheless, episodes that had a shaping influence on
the direction his writing would take. One such occurred in the
fall of 1934, as Warren drove down from Tennessee to assume
his duties at LSU, the former military school that was newly
flourishing under the personal patronage of Huey P. Long:

Along the way I picked up a hitchhiker—a country man, the kind you call a red-neck or a wool-hat, aging, aimless, nondescript, beat up by life and hard times and bad luck, clearly tooth-broke and probably gut-shot, standing beside the road in an attitude that spoke of infinite patience and considerable fortitude, holding a parcel in his hand, wrapped in old newspaper and tied with binder twine, waiting for some car to come along. He was, though at the moment I did not sense it, a mythological figure.[58]

Warren's passenger was an incarnation of the deprivation and resentment Huey Long translated into power. He presented, through no fault of his own, a challenge to democratic institutions. Warren tells us that he made use of this "nameless old hitchhiker" when he came to write of the Dustbowl refugee Jack Burden picks up on his way back from California in *All the King's Men*, but the influence of this human powder keg on his imagination did not begin or end there. In a very real sense, this hitchhiker—an archetype of American folklore, especially the folklore of the Depression—is a presence forever hovering in the background of Warren's first three published novels, books that analyze from different vantage points the relationship between the yearnings of the individual and the mechanics of power politics. Warren's forlorn traveler appears in various guises, some benign and some malignant, but when he speaks—through word or action—author and reader alike listen, for his is the vox populi that will not be ignored.

4

Democracy and "Soulcraft"

Near the beginning of *Night Rider,* Warren's protagonist Percy Munn arrives in the tobacco-trading center of Bardsville aboard a railroad car densely packed with men who have come together in the hope of making a better life for themselves and their families. They want a fair price for their crop, which is to say that they have come to claim what the promise of America assures them is theirs by right—justice. A man of the law and himself a grower, Mr. Munn wants what his fellow passengers want, but he is set off from them by virtue of education and status. *He* is a gentleman, and the stench of stale sweat and whiskey sickens him. In claustrophobic revulsion, he resents the "pressure that was human because it was made by human beings, but was inhuman, too, because you could not isolate and blame any one of those human beings who made it."[1] When Munn steps off the train, he finds the streets of Bardsville crowded as never before with people who "all seemed strangers to him" (*NR* 3). Something will happen, however, that will, for a time at least, bridge the gap between "Mr." Munn and these "strangers." Unexpectedly called upon to address the crowd, he fumbles for clichés until his gaze meets that of "a lanky, stooped man of about fifty, wearing faded blue overalls and a straw hat":

The man's red-rimmed, dull eyes were fixed directly upon him. Then, at that instant, he realized with a profound force that that man there was an individual person, not like anybody else in the world. He realized the fact more profoundly than he had ever realized it about his friends or even his wife; and he saw as clearly as in a vision that man sitting with other men before a small blaze of sticks on which something was cooking, in the dark in the open field, just as Captain Todd had said the people had camped the night before. [*NR* 25]

Munn's words are now invested with meaning. He can articulate the "idea" that has brought these men together and affirm with certitude that there is only hope for the individual when individuals think and act collectively.

Such a transforming confrontation between a Warren protagonist and the Other occurs with a suggestive frequency in his writing,[2] but here its implications are especially revealing. Munn's eloquence, his capacity for leadership, indeed his whole sense of purpose, are derived from the country man in the crowd. In return, Munn provides the silent man with a voice and a vision that give structure to his otherwise incommunicable aspirations. Each man alone is inarticulate and impotent; together they can act in an effort to make the vision real. They are joined in a political symbiosis, the beginnings of what social theorists might term a "collectivity," though one in which leaders and the led are mutually necessary components.[3]

At least from the Age of Reason on, modern forms of government, whether totalitarian or democratic, have claimed a legitimacy that emanates from the collective will of the governed. German Fascism represented itself as the natural expression of the *Volk* spirit fulfilling its historical and biological destiny. Marxist socialism bases its authority on the promise of an ultimate dictatorship of the proletariat. Democracy, the oldest of the three models of social polity dominant in our time, has assumed its justification based on the plebiscite. Its legitimacy is conferred upon the state by the individual citizen, acting in concert with a majority of like-minded peers. Democracy, ideally, aims at consensus arrived at through the workings of a responsible and responsive electorate. It is, Warren would always insist, a process fraught with uncertainties and perils.

Warren's first three published novels (at least two apprentice novels were abandoned by the author) are dramatic studies in the dynamics of political power.[4] They explore the inherent threats that plague a democratic social order, threats implicit in the assumptions behind democratic theory. In these books, Warren brings his probing imagination to bear on fundamental issues that remain unsettled and continue to haunt the American body politic. Taken together, *Night Rider* (1939), *At Heaven's Gate* (1943), and *All the King's Men* (1946) move sequentially from dark skepticism to guarded hope, a hope without guarantees. There is a teleology at work in Warren's vision of democratic process, but it is not necessarily a reassuring one: we get what we deserve. In the grammar of Warren's politics, "the people" can never be more than the plural form of "the person." Thus, his investigations into the nature of American democracy and the dangers it generates out of itself hinge upon the interplay between the will of the one and the will of the many. The claims of individual conscience and consciousness and the aims of a volatile collectivity are woven together in a necessarily flawed social fabric.

Warren's debut as a novelist took place in one of the most trying years of the twentieth century, 1939, a year forever fixed in the literary imagination by W.H. Auden:

> Waves of anger and fear
> Circulate over the bright
> And darkened lands of the earth,
> Obsessing our private lives;
> The unmentionable odour of death
> Offends the September night.[5]

In the United States, the Depression lingered on. Though the New Deal had managed to weather the winds of radical change and stay the course of representative democracy, pockets of bitter unrest remained. But any domestic threat to the stability of free institutions was negligible in the face of Axis expansionism. The surge of the blitzkrieg was plunging Europe into darkness. In the words of Tennessee Williams's Tom Wingfield, "Nowadays the world is lit with lightning."[6]

It would be futile to deny the critical truism that *Night Rider* is, like all of Warren's novels, a "philosophical" fiction involving questions of identity and awareness, the defining of self through thought and action, and the nature of the good. Like the literature the New Critics valued most, it resists relegation to the status of a cultural artifact. Still, *Night Rider* had a special relevance for readers at the time it was published, and it is important to try to recapture something of that aspect of the work. When Christopher Isherwood saw in Percy Munn a type of the "tragic liberal,"[7] he placed *Night Rider* in both a literary and a political context, a context that was accepted as a given some years later by Irene Hendry, who discussed Warren's first two novels in a pioneering essay that appeared, significantly enough, at the conclusion of World War II. From her perspective in time, Hendry understood the intimate connection Warren's novel shared with the "revolutionary" fiction of the Left, more particularly with the novels of intellectually sophisticated rebels like André Malraux, and she also regarded the career of Percy Munn as an accurate projection of modern "political man," that individual who so easily assumed the role of "soldier" in "a modern mechanized army" or "citizen" in "a totalitarian state."[8]

Night Rider may have obvious ties to European novels like those of Malraux, and it certainly bears favorable comparison with later fiction by engaged existentialists like Sartre and Camus, but the power politics it explores are indigenously American, and reminiscent of the War for Independence. The agrarian revolt Warren chronicles is spearheaded by a propertied class. Mr. Munn, the lawyer, is recruited by the substantial landholder Bill Christian, and his peers on the Board of the Association of Growers of Dark Fired Tobacco are men of standing in the community, men known to mind the main chance. Small growers and even tenants are essential to the success of the association; their stake in the outcome is proportionately less but just as real. In this connection, the very title "association" is particularly apt and more than a little suggestive.

Visiting the United States during the rambunctious administration of Andrew Jackson, Alexis de Tocqueville wondered at Americans' propensity for banding together in "associations"—though he found some of them (notably temperance societies) rather perplexing. Tocqueville regarded associations in America as peculiarly benign, a consequence of "universal suffrage" and a preference for persuasion over coercion, but today his assessment of the positive role they played seems atypically naive: "Political associations in the United States are . . . peaceful in their intentions, and strictly legal in the means which they employ; and they assert with perfect truth, that they only aim at success by lawful means."[9] It is likely that Tocqueville's account of such organizations, though in the main perhaps true, was colored by his deeply felt animus toward Old World factionalism, and his sunny description of active special interest groups in the United States may have elements of the wish-fulfillment fantasy about it, for Tocqueville's more intimate acquaintance with European associations had bred in him an unequivocal distrust:

The greater part of Europeans look upon an association as a weapon which is to be hastily fashioned, and immediately tried in conflict. A society is formed for discussion, but the idea of impending action prevails in the minds of those who constitute it: it is, in fact, an army; and the time given to parley serves to reckon up the strength and to inspire the troops, after which they march against the enemy. Resources which lie within the bounds of the law may suggest themselves to the persons who compose it as a means, but never as the only means, of success.[10]

These pernicious associations "centralize the direction of their resources as much as possible, and they entrust the power of the whole party to a very small number of leaders," which has an inevitably corruptive effect upon the remaining rank and file:

The members of these associations reply to a watch word, like soldiers on duty; they profess the doctrine of passive obedience, or rather in uniting together they at once abjure the exercise of their own judgment and free will. And the tyrannical control which these societies exercise, is often far more insupportable than the authority possessed over society by the Government which they attack. Their moral force is much diminished by these excesses.

They lose the sacred quality which always characterizes a struggle between oppressors and the oppressed. The man who in given cases consents to obey his fellows with servility, and who submits his actions and even his opinions to their control, can have no claim to rank as a free citizen.[11]

I cite Tocqueville at length because his analysis of the workings of such sinister associations so accurately prefigures the progress of the tobacco-growers' movement in *Night Rider*, as well as the fate that overtakes Percy Munn. When lawful means lead only to qualified success and when failure looms with increasing probability, the Association of Growers of Dark Fired Tobacco—or rather its board, made up of heretofore respectable pillars of the community—shifts into an extra-legal mindset and adopts a mode of operation that not only connives at but employs paramilitary violence. Warren reveals the seeds of this violence from the beginning. In the drunken rally that follows Munn's speech, the new members of the association revel well into the night, "singing something to the tune of 'John Brown's Body'" (*NR* 28). Brown, no respecter of the civil law, ended as no respecter of persons—no respecter of human life. But the irony here runs deeper. These demonstrators have appropriated for their purposes the southern version of the old Civil War song, with its call to hang John Brown (later Abe Lincoln) "to a sour apple tree" (*NR* 28). (One might ask how Brown's ultimate crime—treason—is different from an intention to lynch the elected president of the United States.) Something has happened to scramble the traditional categories of law, order, and justice in the darkened streets of Bardsville—and in the minds of a free citizenry only concerned (initially) with righting economic wrongs. Hearing the raucous words of the song, Munn thinks that the buyers for the big tobacco companies that have conspired to keep prices low are wise to stay off the streets and out of harm's way, though at this point they need not fear physical molestation. The threat of violence is still high-spirited and jocular, but it is present nonetheless, and when violence does break out it escalates brutally, breeding itself, fueled more and more by instincts considerably baser than a desire for justice. Warren shows how the pursuit of economic self-interest, on its own terms hardly objectionable, can become a stalking horse for darker emotions that, once unleashed, shatter all those psychic and social restraints that make the realization of genuine self-interest possible.[12]

In *Night Rider*, as in all his best fiction, Warren's "truth" emerges through the dialectical interaction of characters' words, actions, and relationships with one another, and thus Senator Tolliver, one of the book's most flawed figures, is nonetheless reliable when he warns Munn early on that "in any popular movement there is a tendency toward extreme action that you don't see" (*NR* 111). The violence growing out of social unrest tends to be sporadic and for the most part latent until a "leader" (*Führer? Duce?*) appears on the scene to release its deadly potential: "They say a ship can burn for days and not much harm done until somebody opens a hatch and the air strikes. A leader is like that, he just opens a hatch" (*NR* 111). Tolliver is speaking here of the threat to the growers' association posed by the volatile Bill Christian, who wants to extract blood as much as money from the buyers. But Mr. Christian's rantings are considerably less dangerous than the ostensibly rational suggestions of Professor Ball and Dr. MacDonald, an ideologue and a strategist respectively, who together activate the terrorist wing of the association and christen it the Free Farmers' Brotherhood of Protection and Control. Behind the euphemism of the title lurks the ominous truth. Munn and his fellows have moved beyond the limits of a voluntary "association" and are now joined together in an irrational intimacy that, quite significantly, approximates ties of blood. These "Free Farmers" surrender any real freedom they might claim once they take an oath to obey unquestioningly the commands of their superiors. In the struggle to acquire what is rightfully theirs, they willingly lose themselves. "Protection" suggests that they are driven to adopt radical measures out of defensive necessity, but the ultimate word in the new organization's title, "control," unmistakably exposes the hunger for domination that lurks beneath the surface and provides its leaders with their reason for being. The brotherhood's motto, *"Le bras pour le droit,"* proclaims its reliance on the wholly amoral principle that might makes right.

At first glance, the ideological underpinnings of the brotherhood, as formulated by Professor Ball, the rural *philosophe,* seem an unlikely rationale for full-blown civil strife. Ball keeps a small classical academy in the best humanistic tradition of the border South. He is, moreover, a *compleat* agrarian, fond of sprinkling his letters to provincial newspapers with quotations from Jefferson and John Taylor of Caroline. Cicero (whose eloquence was so often self-serving and fractious) is another favorite, and indeed Professor Ball's notion of an ideal polity seems to accord with the Roman republican model. In this regard, he invokes the talismanic name of Cincinnatus, a shadowy historical figure of great importance to many of the image-makers of the American Revolution. (The fact that the professor is an intellectual heir of the neoclassicism of the Enlightenment is no accident but rather an important element in Warren's unfolding political critique.)

Ball professes to be "a man of peace" (he later commits a murder for which Percy Munn is blamed), but when circumstances seem to require it he is ready with an argument that justifies any and all means of achieving his desired end, and he is prepared to back up his conclusions with an appeal to authorities of the highest stature: " 'Now what's the right thing one time, that thing the next time is wrong. It's in the Bible that way, and the Stagarite. If I peruse him aright'" (*NR* 142). The Scriptures and the *Nicomachean Ethics* are seldom regarded as forerunners of the situational ethic Professor Ball proposes. He has not read Aristotle "aright" (though Warren has), and his misreading is prompted by inner compulsions that clearly run counter to the Aristotelian virtues of reason, moderation, and restraint. It finally comes as no surprise when the professor takes refuge in religious fanaticism once the collapse of the brotherhood is assured, identifying the farmers' cause with that of the Israelites and equating their enemies (which now include the Commonwealth of Kentucky) with Pharaoh's drowned horsemen and the doomed Canaanites. The failure of

Professor Ball's ideology, itself a betrayal of its own just principles, is now complete.

Ideology may be an indispensable element in the founding of a radical movement, at least during the formative stages, but it soon takes second seat to action, as Tocqueville observed in the 1830s and as Warren makes manifest in *Night Rider*. If Professor Ball is a botched Man Thinking, his son-in-law Dr. MacDonald, the consummate organizer and strategist, is the real force behind the brotherhood and an avowed realist. He is a man of few words, and thus, when he speaks, men listen and are predisposed to act. If the doctor has a reigning passion, it is his unswerving commitment to discipline and, ironically, an adherence to authority—his authority. With his seemingly unshakable good humor and distanced self-control, he is ultimately as effective a seducer of the wills of others as Senator Tolliver, who prefers to follow the more customary path of insinuation, flattery, and shammed sincerity. Dr. MacDonald understands the mechanics of human weakness and inconstancy well enough, but how "realistic" a man is he? His past remains obscure, but there are frequent reminders in the text that he once took part in some thwarted form of foreign adventurism in Mexico. Is he wiser as a result? Seeking to reassure Munn that the setbacks suffered by the growers need not prove fatal, he makes a disarming admission—the significance of which is lost on Warren's protagonist, who is by this point utterly self-deluded: " 'A man don't need much in a pinch. It'll surprise you, by God. I lived once, six weeks it was, on just a handful of parched corn a day and a jack rabbit or a prairie chicken when I could get one, and me on the move, too. Moving fast. . . . That was down in Mexico.' " (*NR* 330). By the end of the novel, it is Percy Munn, Warren's modern "political man," who is running for his life.

In a sense, Munn, like so many Warren characters, has been in headlong flight from the start. He has been a "night rider," careening blindly through the dark of his own alienation.[13] Indeed, it is in seeking to fill the vacuous core of his being that he so willingly surrenders himself to the association and then to the brotherhood. His involvement in the growers' movement affects him like liquor; he is explicitly drunk on power, and a mean drunk at that. Nowhere is the perversity of Munn's psychic state more dramatically apparent than in the scene where he rapes his wife, May. This passage, though briefly rendered, is all the more shocking, eclipsing in brutality the bungled murder of Bunk Trevelyan that immediately precedes it, for unlike the murder, a confused and ambiguous act, Munn's assault on his unoffending wife is an act of cold and pitiless aggression.

Appalling at the most literal level, this turn in the narrative is no less important symbolically. Traditionally, marriage is thought of as the primal social contract, an institution that channels the otherwise disruptive procreational urge in a positive direction. Out of this basic accommodation between the lower and higher aspects of the human creature comes the possibility of a society devoted to the commonweal. Munn, the man of law, has violated both the letter and the spirit of civil statutes already. Evidence he obtains without a search warrant hangs an innocent man and frees a guilty client, Trevelyan. Munn then takes personal responsibility for eliminating this same client, who has betrayed the brotherhood, on the very night he defiles May. Such lawless excess might be mitigated by arguing that the association and brotherhood constitute a law (of sorts) unto themselves. But the rape of May, though Warren has subtly prepared the reader for it,[14] is a ferocious attack upon human communion, in effect a blasphemous denial of natural law. When Munn later learns that May is pregnant, he is troubled by a dream that is profoundly emblematic. His wife comes to him, "a great sweetness, but a sadness" in her face, and presents him with something wrapped in a newspaper that crumbles at his touch. The bundle contains a fetus with the face of Bunk Trevelyan; it is "alive" and strains "to speak" to Munn. But May begins to laugh instead, and Munn, "with a coldness of calculation," wants to strike out to halt that laughter, lest "everything would shrivel and be blotted out and devoured, and there would be nothing but that soundless ferocity of laughter and himself alone in the midst of it" (NR 395-96). There is no more compelling index to Munn's perdition. The political and personal poles of his damnation meet here.

In a very real sense, *Night Rider* may be said to begin where so much of the protest literature of the 1930s left off.[15] In the drama and fiction of social protest, great suffering breeds solidarity and hope. This hope hinges upon collective action. At the conclusion of the quintessential proletarian play, Clifford Odets's *Waiting for Lefty* (1935), the union is ready to strike. In Steinbeck's *The Grapes of Wrath*, published the same year as Warren's first novel,[16] the loner Tom Joad, whose only obligations have been the ties of kin, comes to embrace the whole family of man, claiming a messianic oneness with the dispossessed and exploited throughout the world. Percy Munn and the little people for whom he speaks yearn for a similar deliverance, but they succeed only in laying, in the sharecropper Mr. Grimes's words, "a curse . . . onto the land" (*NR* 257). Warren emphatically suggests that radical action, with its tendency to proliferate rather than curb suffering, is only to be pursued at our own peril. Born out of desperation, it is more often than not an enemy rather than an instrument of hope. What makes its destructive nature so apparent in Warren's novel is, of course, the *fact* of failure. Shared danger and hardship bring out virtues as well as vices in Warren's principal characters, virtues like perseverance, loyalty, and courage: *civic* virtues. The movement to which Munn and the others pledge their "sacred" honor may be quixotic, but we regard it as such *only* because it does not succeed. Here the implied parallels between the leaders of the brotherhood and the Fathers of the Republic are most telling. A failed revolution cannot conceal the darker forces it has unleashed, forces a successful revolutionary enterprise sublimates into acts of heroism and martyrdom.[17] In a sense, Warren is addressing himself in *Night Rider* to moral issues that a pietistic historiography traditionally ignores. The American nation had a violent, disorderly, and bloody birthing. What are the implications of this fact? How has it left its mark on our past and present? What future can be built on such awareness? These questions are submerged in *Night Rider*, and the author does not presume to answer them. As we have seen, Warren is suspicious of any answer that pretends to be definitive, but that does not abolish the need to question. Rather, it means that the questioning must never cease.

Yet, one conclusion emerges for certain, and Warren drives the point home by focussing upon the individual, not the collectivity, at the end: political commitment alone is an inadequate surrogate for a holistic sense of one's interpenetration with the world.[18] Percy Munn's political life began when he gave voice to the desires of a nameless country man in the crowd at Bardsville; when it is over, it is Munn who attends to the vernacular wisdom of another such man, Willie Proudfit, who was also present in the crowd. In the vast theater of the American West—here, as elsewhere in Warren's writing, a state of consciousness as well as a geographical realm—Proudfit has acted out a fabulistic paradigm of our national experience. He tells a tale of promise turned against itself, of hope perverted by greed, bloodlust, and a strangely mechanistic eagerness to war against the natural order.

Proudfit attains a redemptive vision in the West. He has undergone a version of that "regeneration through violence" Richard Slotkin has identified as one of America's defining mythic motifs.[19] But, significantly, the world Willie Proudfit returns to is not redeemed. He will, we are led to believe, lose the home of his heart's desire—his mortgaged farm. Nor should we assume that Proudfit's vision immunizes him from deadly error. He too has come under the charismatic influence of Dr. MacDonald, and the murder of the witness his guest Munn is accused of killing meets with his tacit approbation. Still, Proudfit is blessed with a decidedly un-Emersonian brand of self-reliance, an inner peace and affirmative certainty of the kind Munn had sought to find by committing himself unstintingly to the brotherhood. Something of Proudfit's hard-won humanity would seem to have been unconsciously assimilated by Warren's dehumanized and dehumanizing protagonist, who backs off from his intention to assassinate Senator Tolliver at the novel's close. Munn may have killed men, directly or indirectly, in the past, but he is no killer in the end.

Is it possible that Munn has, in his final moments, morally (and "politically") come of age?[20] Dying, he hears the voices of his pursuers, "calling emptily, like the voices of boys at a game in the dark" (*NR* 460). This image of child's play is a recurring one in *Night Rider*. Indeed, there is a Tom Sawyer quality, a ludic dimension, to the lethal game the brotherhood has undertaken to play with its enemies, a game replete with passwords, secret oaths, grand gestures, and deeds of vainglory. Quite significantly, it is a game a fully individuated man like Warren's Captain Todd (who played out a similar game for all it was worth during and after the Civil War) disdains to join.

The professed aim of power politics is what Aristotle termed the "good," in social terms the *commonweal*, but Warren demonstrates throughout his "political" novels that power brokers, themselves often driven by a sense of their own incompleteness, want something more—control, of others and the entire field of play. In this regard, we might do well to consider the obsessive appeal of the board game Monopoly, born in and of the Great Depression, for it exposes in its devotees something of the aggression and ruthlessness of the financial system it burlesques. Its object is domination; its motives, to use a highly-charged Warrenesque adjective, are "pure."

If *Night Rider* is properly understood as Warren's response to the literature of social protest, his second novel, *At Heaven's Gate*, clearly belongs in the company of those works that radically challenge the American ethic of success and, in doing so, call into question the beneficent claims of corporate and finance capitalism. (There is a direct, if highly adulterated, line of descent linking this tradition with perennially popular television series like *Dallas, Falcon Crest,* and *Dynasty*.) In *Night Rider*, Warren purposely confers upon the big tobacco conglomerates a measure of invisibility, even as he shows how their influence is ubiquitous and palpable. In *At Heaven's Gate*, he reverses the process, immersing his readers in the plutocratic world of high finance, unscrupulous speculation, and the cynical undermining of political and personal integrity in the name of profit. It is a world founded upon fraudulent assumptions about the nature of value and the value of nature.

Two of Warren's most astute critics, James H. Justus and Richard G. Law, have touched upon the "Agrarian" critique of liberal capitalism at work in the novel,[21] and unquestionably *I'll Take My Stand* and *Who Owns America?* can provide a useful gloss on setting, character, and symbolism in *At Heaven's Gate.* But it is John L. Longley, Jr., who, in an essay published over a quarter of a century ago, has perhaps best traced the ideological superstructure of the novel and analyzed its indictment of the "managerial age,"[22] that age (with us now more than ever) in which style replaces substance, consumption supersedes communion, and the "self" is a marketplace commodity.

The residual strength of Longley's reading is a direct result of the rigor with which he applies to the text Warren's admission that *At Heaven's Gate* owes both its conception and its realization to an intensive study of Dante.[23] With precious few exceptions, all the characters who people the pages of Warren's book are consigned to the Seventh Circle, that precinct of Hell reserved for those who have sinned against natural law. Catholic Christianity has never been comfortable with the social and economic implications of capitalism, based as it is on the *unnatural* system of "usury," the meretricious generation of wealth apart from *real* goods and services, a making of something out of nothing that abuses God's plenitude. In the eyes of the British Distributists, fellow travelers of the Agrarians in the 1930s, "usury" was capitalism's greatest sin, a notion that Ezra Pound, anything but a Catholic, made much of in his *Cantos:*

> Usura slayeth the child in the womb
> It stayeth the young man's courting
> It hath brought palsey to bed, lyeth
> between the young bride and her bridegroom
> CONTRA NATURAM
> [Canto XLV]

Warren's overview of a society poisoned by the presence of Bogan Murdock, the financier who erects an empire on specious "securities," is no less ferocious than Pound's diatribes against Usura. More to the point, its theological dimension is developed in great detail. In *At Heaven's Gate*, it is the *testifying* of Ashby Wyndham, an embodiment of primitive Christian virtues and yet another of Warren's forgotten men whose voice must be heard, that provides us with the moral norm against which Murdock and his world are weighed and found wanting. Indeed, it seems altogether fair to regard *At Heaven's Gate* as Warren's most "orthodox" novel—religiously speaking. It apparently dates from that period in his life when his reading of Dante nearly affected his conversion to the institutional Church: as Warren told Peter Stitt in 1977, "Dante almost got me at one stage."[24] In *Night Rider*, the spiritual referents for judging the politics of violence are made most emphatic through the medium of Willie Proudfit but are largely encapsulated *in* and confined *to* his narrative. In *At Heaven's Gate*, however, the statement of Ashby Wyndham in effect provides a running Judeo-Christian commentary present throughout.[25] Later, in *All the King's Men*, Warren was to handle the "religious" component of his politics somewhat differently, but it would play no less vital a role in his political disquisition there. Whatever Warren may have thought of the contemporary conservative pundit George Will, he too insisted that the well-being of the polis and the spiritual health of the individual citizen are inextricably bound up with one another, so that "statecraft," if it would succeed in implementing "the good," must recognize the importance of "soulcraft."[26]

Warren, like Dante and the patristic fathers before him, recognized that the soul longs for completeness and communion, but these very longings may lead to the lusting after false gods. Both Christianity and Marxism (though it scoffs at the soul) are profoundly aware of the dangers of co-option, the world's way of buying off one's true self-interest by offering a vested interest in the corrupt status quo. Bogan Murdock, who as a boy had been drawn to music as "the only pure thing in the world,"[27] is a virtuosic co-optor, who plays the needs of others like a complicated instrument, drawing out of human discord a dubious and deceptively reassuring harmony. None of the major characters in the novel are exempt from his manipulations, though Murdock's "hegemony" (a privileged term these days) is most often affirmed indirectly.

Creeping co-option takes Private Porsum, the war hero whose reputation makes him a good investment for Murdock, virtually unawares; Porsum holds the key to the mountain people's trust, and at a crucial point that trust is betrayed. Duckfoot Blake, on the other hand, is an accountant for Murdock who from the outset knows the score only too well: the firm of Meyer and Murdock "ain't a business," but rather "the Hindu rope trick" (*AHG* 72). Duckfoot seeks to hide his own not inconsiderable culpability behind a pose of cynical superiority, even as he takes Murdock's pay for services rendered. When his cynicism proves untenable at the novel's conclusion, the damage has already been done, and the degree of his own complicity is apparent. Sue Murdock, the financier's daughter, has been emotionally co-opted from birth, and her pathetic and ineffectual efforts to achieve a measure of autonomy end in a self-destructive spiral that serves as an index of the degree to which she has always remained the dependent child of her ruthless father and the genetic heir of her alcoholic mother. Even Sue's death is turned to Murdock's advantage. Sue's lover, the labor organizer Jason Sweetwater, demonstrates a phenomenon that might be called "inverse" co-option. The son of a superannuated southern clergyman, Sweetwater flees his father's effete and eviscerate Christianity and pursues a life of profligacy until he finds himself (not unlike Percy Munn) through commitment to radical political activity. In a perversely ironic way, Sweetwater is a mere by-product, a creature, of the capitalist system.

Warren delights here in an often-overlooked irony that drives the Marxian engine of history: any meaning radicalism may posit can only arise, proportionately, out of the power of the social institutions it seeks to oppose. Even Slim Sarrett, Warren's distasteful portrait of the modernist artist/intellectual, a man who, like Sweetwater, resembles Murdock in more

ways than one, is fully co-opted, his blistering and insightful
assaults on the capitalist ethic and apparent disdain for all
its works to the contrary. In the novel's final chapter, Sarrett
is reduced to little more than a parody of Bogan Murdock
when he checks into a grand hotel in New York on the money
he takes from Sue's purse after strangling the girl whose life
had been figuratively choked out of her by her father long
before.

Our final glimpse of Sarrett in the hotel room significantly
recalls a similar scene in the opening chapter, in which Jerry
Calhoun, the novel's central figure, sits in his hotel at the
conclusion of a successful business trip to New York as Murdock's representative. The hotel is, of course, a metaphorical
device Warren often employs, a symbol of the transient en-
vironment of modernity, a place of hired comfort, a poor travesty of home. Jerry seems to sense this and makes a pathetic
attempt to communicate on a more human basis with the
bellboy, only to have his overtures misinterpreted and re-
buffed.[28] A former football All-American who once found in his
study of geology a kind of poetry of the earth but soon, under
Murdock's influence, trades in that vision for a new one in
which the rocks of ages are reenvisioned as "resources" (*AHG*
130), Jerry is the prototypical "all-American boy," rising from
humble roots to increasing affluence and the prestige that
accompanies it. His rise and fall most obviously expose the
sometimes subtle, but always violent, attack upon integrity
(personal and political) that co-option entails. Jerry, like Duckfoot Blake and Jason Sweetwater, would like to think of himself as a self-made man, but in reality he has bought into a
system in which the self is unmade and unmanned.

The game of football, significantly, is Jerry's entree into that
more heady game Murdock plays with such mastery.[29] Jerry is
to a degree a victim of Murdock the Hustler, but he has unconsciously played the game of success almost from the beginning, all the while deceiving himself about his motives. When
he is asked to pledge an unfashionable fraternity in college, he
declines, using his lack of money as a rationale. Nevertheless,
when the opportunity to join the most prestigious fraternity

on campus presents itself, he does so, though a wealthy alum-
nus (Murdock perhaps?) must pay his dues. Jerry is only the
most visible of the young men Murdock diverts from useful
careers in the sciences or medicine, assembling them in yet
another fraternity, Meyers and Murdock, where they all speak
"the same language" and wear "the same clothes," serving
loyally as Murdock's young "proconsuls" (*AHG* 67).

The designation "proconsul" is a suggestive one, for there is
in *At Heaven's Gate*, as in *Night Rider*, a kind of historical
subtext that centers on ancient Rome. Whereas Professor Ball
in the earlier novel alludes with unsuspecting irony to Cincinnatus, Bogan Murdock quite fittingly quotes the bloody and
perverted emperor Tiberius, whom he regards, altogether out
of context, as "noble" (*AHG* 109).[30] The implicit yet insistent
presence of the Matter of Rome in Warren's second novel functions as a submerged gloss on character and action and by
associative extension quietly suggests to the reader the degree
to which the new cash-nexus imperialism of twentieth-century
America has supplanted the classical republican ideal of the
Founders. Murdock finds Jerry Calhoun worth investing in
partly because Jerry is distantly related to a former governor
of the state who represents, in Duckfoot Blake's words, a time
"when every politician was a Roman statesman and the *res
publica* was untainted" (*AHG* 111). Such a time, of course, is the
political equivalent of the Golden Age, a myth, but not a
worthless one if embraced in the right spirit. Murdock, however, is less interested in cultivating the spirit of patrician
leadership than in acquiring its outward mantle.

Murdock's father ran for governor years before but killed his
opponent in cold blood for telling the truth about the Murdock
family's scalawaggery during the Civil War. Family "honor" is
but a rationale for this act of unmitigated criminality, an act
that rouses Jerry Calhoun's malignant Uncle Lew to irrational
(if not altogether unreasonable) outbursts of righteous indig-
nation.[31] The need to purchase respectability helps explain
Bogan Murdock's later marriage to Dorothy Hopewell (with
her significant surname), whose great-great-grandfather was a
general in the Revolutionary War and whose grandfather was a

senator in the Confederacy. (Ironically, there is no taint attached to the fact that the Hopewell family had owned human
chattel.) Dorothy's "dowry" is meager in terms of tangible
treasure, bringing Murdock only "a small, heavily encumbered
property," but it is more than adequate for Murdock's needs,
for he is adept at turning intangibles like the Hopewell reputation to tangible gain. Through marriage, Murdock also assumes possession of the great-great-grandsire's "Revolutionary sword," which comes to hang in Murdock's library. We are
pointedly told by Warren that the old man's boots "had long
since rotted away in a family attic" (*AHG* 187). It is just as well;
there is no one in *At Heaven's Gate* capable of filling them.

General Hopewell's sword, a tool of revolution, symbolizing
a willingness to utilize force in the interest of meaningful
change, is more than simply another decorative object in Murdock's elegant library. It proclaims Murdock's desire to employ
for profit (psychic much more than pecuniary) the vestiges of a
heroic past, albeit a past more imagined than real, in which
the self and the social order reinforced one another sym-
biotically. As it is, Murdock feeds parasitically upon the body
politic; his unhealthy influence invades virtually every aspect
of the social organism. But he is not, as some critics have
implied,[32] a one-dimensional villain. Warren once praised
Hemingway for daring to portray the human face of fascism in
For Whom the Bell Tolls,[33] and he takes pains to do the same
thing for Murdock in *At Heaven's Gate*. Murdock's humanity,
complex and undeniable though warped, surfaces in a number
of indirect but compelling ways—in the sad little tune he
improvises on the piano, in Sue's poignant memories of her
father as the gentle "Dockie," in Murdock's solicitous loyalty to
his senile father (whose stigma marked him as a boy and no
doubt contributed to making him the moral grotesque he is).
As Duckfoot Blake reminds the reader throughout the novel,
Bogan Murdock is a "dream" of his own making, and he man-
ages to exist only by lying to himself, insisting that high finance is "not abstract": "its only function is to answer the
needs of the land itself and the life which is dictated by the
nature of our land" (*AHG* 56). Likewise, Murdock the exploiter

can assert without apparent irony that the dehumanizing system he represents operates in the best interest of those it exploits: "If they could only see where their interest lies. That co-operation is best" (*AHG* 222). Murdock has devoted his public career to assembling the props of the good life, but the truly good life (in every sense) has always eluded him, as he reveals in an offhanded way when he imagines "taking a year off" to see emerging China as it confronts "the world of industry and finance and science." The mystic East represents an alternate world, "complete in its own terms, and wise." There, Murdock believes, it might be possible for him to "see himself a little more clearly" (*AHG* 221).

The British critic Marshall Walker, perhaps somewhat ungraciously, has pointed out a parallel between Bogan Murdock and a relatively recent figure in American history, Richard Nixon.[34] Indeed, the closing scene in the novel, a press conference where Murdock takes responsibility—*but not blame*—for the fiasco he has precipitated, seems remarkably prescient of Watergate. But despite the "courage" and dignity Murdock seeks to convey, the utter emptiness of his pose before the camera is apparent, as is his absurdly ahistorical attempt to identify himself with yet another president of the United States, whose portrait, "large as life," hangs above his library mantle: "It is the portrait of a man who, more than a century ago, endured cold and hunger, who killed men with his own hand, who survived steaming malarial swamps and long marches, who was ruthless, vindictive, cunning, and headstrong, who was president of his country, who died in the admiration, or hatred, of millions of men. There is the painted face: the sunken flesh over the grim jawbone, the deep, smoldering eyes, the jutting beak of a nose, and the coarse crest of grayish hair, like an old cockatoo" (*AHG* 391). This is the "painted face" of Andrew Jackson, who, in his war against the Bank and sometimes violent championship of little men like Ashby Wyndham and Jerry Calhoun's father, represents all that is the antithesis of Murdock and his minions. Warren's "portrait" of Murdock and his family is all the more ironic. Murdock's gesture toward the Jacksonian image is thus an unconscious act of self-indictment, and Murdock is subject to a fittingly Dantesque justice. Cut off from a vital, if morally ambiguous, past, he exists only in terms of images and symbols that have lost their sustaining force. Murdock has himself been co-opted by a fraudulent system. But, significantly, he has not been rendered harmless, and is less to be pitied than feared.

In the long run, Warren's later work insists, the vacuous promises of Bogan Murdock's version of the American dream are more of a threat to a genuinely democratic social order than either the civil chaos of *Night Rider* or the dictatorial powers of a strongman like Willie Stark, the Boss in *All the King's Men*. As we saw at the outset of this study, Warren believes that nations, no less than the men and women who compose them, must have "myths" to live by, for without vision the social fabric unravels. The danger, symbolized in this closing scene in which Mr. Murdock meets the press, is that the vital myths of the "past"—vital provided they mirror honestly the ironies of our fallible humanity—may be altogether supplanted by the insubstantial *media images* of the present. If that happens, a possibility that haunts Warren's writing with increased anxiety in his later career, America may in the last analysis have no soul to lose, and "freedom" may be little more than a euphemism for enslavement, possibilities that plagued writers as different as Whitman and Melville in the nineteenth century. It is no accident that the protagonist of Warren's next novel is a newspaperman turned political operative, who finally sets about freeing himself only when he is prepared to resume his proper role—that of a "student" and a maker "of history."

If *At Heaven's Gate* may be said to conclude with what we term today a "media event," *All the King's Men* for all practical purposes begins where Warren's second novel leaves off. Accompanied by a full complement of pressmen, Governor Willie Stark and his entourage of political insiders descend on Mason City and the governor's boyhood home. At the end of the novel, in keeping with the symmetry Warren's fiction often employs,

Willie is ready to come home to his estranged wife Lucy—until an assassin's bullet intervenes. But this initial homecoming is another matter. There is nothing personal about it. It is strictly a question of politics. Willie Stark returns to his father's house not out of pious respect for the old man, nor out of sentimental attachment to the hard-scrabble soil that nurtured his early life. Willie implies that these are his motives when he (reluctantly?) addresses the townspeople on the square, but the reader is soon disabused. Indeed, the crowd who hears Willie is a large one, for it is a Saturday—trading day for rural folk—and the governor has scheduled his foray into friendly territory so as to maximize its effectiveness. His trip home is, in the parlance of 1980s campaigning, a "photo op," part of the packaging of Governor Stark, the Boss, the champion of the little man. Likewise, though Willie's remarks in Mason City purport to be extemporaneous, they are unfailingly pointed and pithy—what we would recognize today as polished "sound bytes."

On one level, Willie Stark is a two-dimensional image, rather like the photograph of him, "about six times life size,"[35] that hangs behind the counter in the drugstore. Old Malaciah Wynn, who has known Willie since he was a boy, significantly remarks, "Yore pitcher, . . . hit don't do you no credit, Willie" (*AKM* 7). Indeed, it doesn't, for Willie Stark is one of Warren's most complex characters. Despite the skill with which he wears the mask of an uncouth and unabashed populist demagogue, wielding like a weapon an inflammatory rhetoric in which holy writ and earthy humor combine, there is deep within the governor a reforming idealist trying to assert himself against the shifting, but always constrictive and reductive, roles the modern American politician seems fated to play. The tragic irony of Willie's career is that he cannot seem to "do credit" to his better self and successfully achieve the goals his political vision dictates. As Willie reiterates in varying terms throughout the novel, bricks for building the social edifice must themselves be formed out of the material at hand, and the politics he practices—the inherently duplicitous politics of image—seems not only appropriate but virtually unavoidable in an America where the bogus has replaced the authentic, where West Texas cowboys flock to Gene Autry movies, California bungalows ape Moorish palaces, gas stations resemble "Anne Hathaway's cottage" (*AKM* 270, 312), and life increasingly imitates the advertisements in slick magazines. Willie has little choice but to pursue his dream of social justice in a world where things are not what they seem, where appearance becomes reality or at least effectively usurps reality's claims on the collective mind of the electorate. In fact, the voters in *All the King's Men* hunger for the deceptive image, often preferring it to a disquieting truth. The governor's womanizing, for instance, is no secret (political power is, after all, a recognized aphrodisiac), and he is estranged from his wife, Lucy, even as he poses with her in photographs cynically designed to evoke in the citizenry "a nice warm glow of complacency" (*AKM* 328) in which a knowing disbelief can be willingly suspended. Willie once made the mistake of overestimating the public's appetite for the unadorned truth, in his first gubernatorial campaign, when he discovered that facts, tables of figures, and policy statements only serve to promote voter disaffection and apathy. He is hardly to be blamed if he refuses to repeat the same mistake twice.

Having, through blackmail, successfully staved off impeachment at the hands of a venal legislature controlled by special interests, Willie tells the throng of his supporters, made up largely of the tattered and dispossessed poor whose needs previous administrations have ignored, "Your will is my strength" and "Your need is my justice" (*AKM* 262), but in truth his attitude toward the common people in the aggregate, like his attitude toward himself as their defender, is painfully ambivalent and anything but naively idealistic. In a revealing moment early in the novel, Willie likens his political pandering to the hopes and fears of the voters to slopping hogs, pouring out "swill," to which Jack Burden, with customary sarcasm, replies, "Well, . . . swill is what they live on, isn't it?" (*AKM* 31).

The evidence in the bulk of Warren's fiction, and in much of his poetry, points toward an affirmative response to Jack's rhetorical question, and however much it may pain the sensibilities of egalitarian readers, the fact that Warren deeply distrusted, and often scorned, the general populace must be faced squarely. Hugh Ruppersburg is right to point out that, while Warren might portray humble individuals like Willie Proudfit and Ashby Wyndham with insight and compassion, showing them to be in many ways morally superior to their social betters, he tended to present the common run of humanity as little more than a mob, frequently on the verge of riot.[36] This is only too obviously the case in *Night Rider* and in *At Heaven's Gate*, in which Duckfoot Blake describes the would-be lynchers gathered outside the jail at the novel's conclusion as "the seed of democracy" (*AHG* 371), and Warren included ghastly scenes of rioting in later novels like *Band of Angels* (1955) and *Wilderness* (1961). Some future "new historicist" will no doubt one day write an article indicting Warren on this score, seeing him as a crypto-apologist for an oppressive elitist power structure, but if so Warren will be in good company indeed, for his dread of mob rule is in a tradition of American writing that includes authors as diverse as Cooper, Hawthorne, Melville, Twain, and Faulkner.

Warren may have regarded the "seed of democracy" as unpromising and profoundly flawed, but his commitment to the democratic ideal, in *All the King's Men* and throughout his work, remained intact.[37] Unlike Tate, there is never in Warren's work a flirtation with an aristocratic order along the lines of T.S. Eliot, and for all his sense of the ambiguous legacy of Jeffersonianism, Warren could never have written a book like Pound's bizarre *Jefferson and/or Mussolini*, for there are no supermen in Warren's world. *All the King's Men* hardly presents the elitist politics of characters like Judge Irwin and Governor Stanton as a preferable alternative to Willie Stark's corrupt populism, whatever egregious abuses the latter lends itself to. Warren resembles in sensibility John Adams, and his great-grandsons Henry and Brooks, far more than he does Jefferson, for Warren shared Adams's vestigial awareness of human depravity, yet he was even more consistent than Adams in applying this assumption to the problem of democratic rule.

For Warren, an American ruling class, whether composed of a propertied elite or a Jeffersonian "aristocracy of talent," could not be depended upon to establish and preserve a just and stable social order because those individuals who attain privileged status are quite as susceptible to the dangerous impulses of man's fallen nature as are the unsophisticated and unruly masses they would govern. Willie Stark, more than his predecessors in the earlier novels, Dr. MacDonald and Bogan Murdock, seems to recognize this truth about himself, as symbolized by his decision to turn to his wife Lucy, the "light," [38] at the novel's conclusion.

Willie has been sorely chastened, and made wiser, by experience. Had he lived, "things might have been all different" (*AKM* 400). Because "history is blind, but man is not" (*AKM* 436), they may be different yet. I see more cause for hope, however problematic, at the conclusion of *All the King's Men* than does John Burt.[39] The hope Warren offers is tenuous, but nonetheless present. Indeed, what the author seems to be showing us in the final pages is the possibility of meaningful and positive political action in a democratic context. Jack Burden, who has always run from responsibility, both intellectually and emotionally, is, even as he stands on the brink of World War II, determined to tackle the "awful responsibility" (*AKM* 438) of his moment in history.[40] It has been suggested that a suitable alternative title to *All the King's Men* might be "The Education of Jack Burden," and the education of Jack Burden is the process out of which Robert Penn Warren's ideal American citizen is formed.

As the story of Jack Burden unfolds, two powerful streams, the historical past and the lived present, converge and move inexorably toward a revelation and rebirth that is finally the equivalent of a religious conversion in which the "sick soul" of a representative modern man, alienated, skeptical, and vulnerable, is made whole.[41] It might be going too far to argue that *All the King's Men* is a theodicy, but it does literally present a synoptic theodicy in its closing pages, in the form of a religious tract the Scholarly Attorney dictates to Jack Burden, and while the novel may not presume fully to justify the ways of

God to man it does absolve God from blame for mankind's long history of self-betrayals and failures. In Warren's world, as in Eliot's *Four Quartets*, "Sin is Behovely," but that is only part of the picture. Warren cannot share Eliot's faith that "All shall be well, and / All manner of thing shall be well"[42] any more than he can accept the cold comfort of naturalistic determinism (what Jack refers to as the theory of the Great Twitch). His assertation of Free Will is more radical, and far more demanding than that. Our fate, personal and political, is in our hands. Given mankind's propensity for error, the American promise of a society where human potential is maximized can hardly be counted upon to fulfill itself. Any fulfillment must come about from the other direction, from the bottom up; the formation and maintenance of a society of equity and self-liberation must begin with the efforts, of necessity dogged and gradual, of individuals like Jack Burden, who are "free" only because they recognize that an absolute and unconditional freedom of the "self" is neither possible nor, in the last analysis, desirable. Jack Burden comes into possession of his full human possibility only after a rigorous and traumatic journey of the spirit, at the end of which stands the humbling *and* exhilarating truth that we can never be truly alone, for the paradox of the human condition is that we are one in our shared alienation, anxiety, and weaknesses.

Along the road to Jack Burden's acceptance of his own common humanity and his willingness to assume the social responsibility such knowledge makes imperative, there are numerous episodes and events that point him on his way. They range from the lessons he learns from history through his deepening meditations on the narrative of Cass Mastern to the shocks he sustains from an evolving "history" lived firsthand, most obviously through the deaths of Judge Irwin, Willie Stark, and Adam Stanton. But, in retrospect, perhaps no moment in the novel is more pivotal than Jack's visit to Lucy Stark as an ostensible bearer of bad news. Tom Stark, Lucy and Willie's son, has been accused of impregnating one Sybil Frey, daughter of a minor politico, and Willie's opponents intend to turn this embryonic scandal to their political advantage. Matters are complicated by the fact that "some others—other friends of Sybil" (*AKM* 334) may have as likely a claim on the paternity of the girl's child as Tom. Lucy seems stunned at first by Jack's news, but finally responds in a particularly revealing passage that is itself pregnant with implications:

"It's just a baby," she almost whispered. "It's just a little baby. It's a little baby in the dark. It's not even born yet, and it doesn't know about what's happened. About money and politics and somebody wanting to be a senator. It doesn't know about anything—about how it came to be—about what that girl did—or why—or why the father—why he—" She stopped, and the large brown eyes kept looking at me with appeal and what might have been accusation. Then she said, "Oh, Jack, it's a little baby, and nothing's its fault."

I almost burst out that it wasn't my fault, either, but I didn't.

Then she added, "It may be my grandbaby. It may be my boy's baby."

Then, after a moment, "I would love it." [*AKM* 335-36]

Intertextually, this passage provides a solemn commentary on Sue Murdock's abortion in *At Heaven's Gate*, and, beyond that, hearkens back to the image of Bunk Trevelyan as fetus in Percy Munn's dream in *Night Rider*. More immediately, it calls to mind a familiar passage at the start of *All the King's Men* where Jack Burden philosophizes in a typical vein:

the clammy, sad little foetus which is you way down in the dark which is you too lifts up its sad little face and its eyes are blind, and it shivers cold inside you for it doesn't want to know. . . . It wants to lie in the dark and not know, and be warm in its not-knowing. The end of man is knowledge, but there is one thing he can't know. He can't know whether knowledge will save him or kill him. He will be killed, all right, but he can't know whether he is killed because of the knowledge which he has got or because of the knowledge which he hasn't got and which if he had it, would save him. [*AKM* 9]

The metaphor is "metaphysical" in its complexity, but it clearly points to two suppositions that are vital to understanding the transformation of Jack Burden from cynical loner to engaged citizen. The fetus is the self at its most vulnerable and fundamental level. It is us once all the supportive trappings of social identity are stripped away. It warrants our pity or even, as Lucy would have it, our "love." But the fetus is also pure potentiality, confronting growth and "knowledge," however reluctantly. Put quite simply, it is the incarnation of hope, the embodiment of a future.[43] At the end of the novel, Lucy has claimed Sybil Frey's baby and named him for Willie—an act that openly proclaims her faith in her late husband's ultimate decency, her hope that "things" may indeed be made "different," and her remarkable capacity for an unconditional yet self-empowering love.

Faith, hope, and love—these are the Pauline virtues that Lucy represents, the outward signs of a Christian grace most of the characters in the novel mistake for weakness and a want of worldly sophistication. Chief among these is Jack, who perversely enjoys baiting the Scholarly Attorney in theological discussion, only to accede, in his own fashion, to the old man's assumptions about the relationship of man to God in the book's final pages. Lucy Stark and the Scholarly Attorney share something Jack lacks, a capacity to define themselves through embracing the despised Other; they can love.[44] Love is the thing Jack flees most desperately, denying himself in denying the claims placed upon him in turn by his mother, his supposed father (the Scholarly Attorney), his first wife, Lois, and—until the end—Anne Stanton. His fear of self-surrender ironically robs him of his full selfhood, as he allows a cynical and detached mask to hide his human face and works at the objectifying of others by relegating them to the status of types (the Friend of Your Youth; the Upright Judge, etc.).

When the theory of the Great Twitch briefly absolves Jack of his responsibility toward those his life impinges upon, he enjoys for a time a false sense of "beatitude," but he begins to move toward a truly enlightened, *lucid* state only when he comes to understand that his contempt for ludicrous humanity is at bottom a species of self-contempt; his "sneer" is self-directed (*AKM* 370). An even harder lesson awaits him; Jack must face the loathsome, but ultimately liberating, fact that he is, like Jefferson and R.P.W. in Warren's subsequent "Tale in Verse and Voices," a brother to dragons, more particularly a kind of Siamese twin of the noxious Tiny Duffy:

We were twins bound together more intimately and disastrously than the poor freaks of the midway who are bound by the common stitch of flesh and gristle and the seepage of blood. We were bound together forever and I could never hate him without hating myself or love myself without loving him. We were bound together under the unwinking eye of Eternity and by the Holy Grace of the Great Twitch whom we must all adore.

And I heaved and writhed like the ox or the cat, and the acid burned my gullet and that was all there was to it and I hated everything and everybody and myself and Tiny Duffy and Willie Stark and Adam Stanton. To hell with them all, I said impartially under the stars. They all looked alike to me then. And I looked like them.

That was the way it was for quite a while. [*AKM* 417][45]

But not for good. Like Willie Proudfit, Ashby Wyndham, and Cass Mastern, Jack achieves a new and fundamentally religious perspective on the world and the mortals who travel through it. But the rebirth of Jack Burden differs from that of the earlier characters in both degree and kind. It is less self-contained and quietistic than Proudfit's and much less frantic and compulsive in its consequences than Wyndham's and Mastern's. It is pointedly less pietistic in any conventional sense, but, because of the primacy of love as its informing principle, it is Other-oriented (which is to say action-oriented) to an unprecedented degree. And Jack, significantly, is not compelled to act; his new determination to "go into the convulsion of the world, out of history into history and the awful responsibility of Time" (*AKM* 438) is willed. Only in our commitments are we free.

As a "student of history," Jack Burden comes to accept and act upon one of his creator's most basic working premises: out of the past comes our present and with it the possibility of a future. This is, of course, the assumption that fuels Warren's *retrospective* imagination, with its determined compulsion to connect the *now* with the *then*, to identify history's "line of continuity to us, and *through* us,"[46] a highly speculative process dramatized most nakedly in Warren's great pivotal poem of the 1940s, *The Ballad of Billie Potts*.[47] A meditation on folk history, drawing vividly on the indigenous humor of the Old

Southwest, *Billie Potts* mirrors as well its author's sense of the dangers inherent in modern America's drive to erase the past. Little Billie's flight into the West, like the nation's rush toward the deceptively millennial promise of the future, must end, like it or not, in a return to origins.

In the final analysis, Warren insists, we never cease being what we *were*, even in the process of becoming what we *are* and envisioning what we *might be*. To deny the continuity of past, present, and future is to gamble with the very notion of an integral self—a gamble the individual (or a whole people) is fated to lose. Warren's persistent backward glance in no way conceals an impulse toward regression and evasion. We cannot, his work asserts over and again, anchor ourselves for security's sake to what has been, for to attempt to do so would be to deny what can and should be. But the past can provide us with a set of bearings from which to chart a new and hopefully better course. Warren's writing in the postwar era represents an ongoing experiment in psychic and social navigation.

Renegotiating the Covenant

In 1970, Warren brought out a Reader's Edition of selected verse by Herman Melville, and like most of his ventures into scholarship and criticism, it was an act of self-revelation.[1] In his introduction, he asserted that the Civil War had had a "curative" effect on Melville. More particularly, "what it . . . did for him was to lead him to see that the fate of man is to affirm his manhood by action, even in the face of the difficulty of defining truth." Warren added, "Man to be man must try to comprehend the density and equivocalness of experience but at the same time he must not forfeit the ability to act."[2] Warren's Melville thus emerged as a historical precursor of Jack Burden, whose ultimately affirmative vision of the interplay between human possibilities and liabilities was likewise forged out of pain and tempered with disillusionment.

Warren had conceived *All the King's Men* during a time when "blank power" alone seemed to guide historical process, and the writer's craft appeared increasingly "irrelevant to this unmasking of . . . brute force."[3] In the years leading up to the Second World War, it seemed at times as if "the de-humanizing forces had won" (*Talking* 22), but by the war's conclusion Warren's situation was essentially what he would project upon a Melville a quarter-century later. While in no way downplaying life's paradoxes and moral ambiguities, both Jack Burden and his creator sounded a call to action. *All the King's Men* argued that the battle for the soul of modern man was far from lost and that literature was scarcely "irrelevant" as long as the writer did not abdicate his or her role as citizen/artist, the purveyor of vision and the mediator between what has been, what is, and what yet may be. The poem or novel would always remain for Warren an aesthetic act, but an aesthetic act that had its profoundly social dimension.

In the preceding chapters, I have argued that there was an implicit "prophetic" strain present in Warren's work from the outset.[4] In the postwar years, that prophetic voice grew increasingly emphatic. Though Warren's faith in literature's power to shape history remained qualified, he nevertheless embraced in unequivocal terms a professed calling to "bear an honest witness to my time" (*Talking* 220). As we have seen, Warren's "witness" was grounded upon an unmitigating backward glance. Any meaningful understanding of our present predicament, as independent "selves" and as members of society, begins with what Jack Burden would call "a lesson in history," and all hope for psychic and social amelioration depends upon establishing a dynamic working relationship with the past.

What we might well term Warren's "jeremiad" differs markedly from that of both the Old Testament prophets *and* other American "prophets" of the conventional Right or Left.[5] Since history, read honestly, offers us no model for a Golden Age, to seek to renew in some pristine sense the flawed convenant of the Founders is an exercise in useless sentimentality. But neither would it be wise, Warren insists, to renounce their dream out of hand. However problematic, and indeed subversive, it might be, Warren's piety toward the past was a constant. What he called America to was not a simplistic renewal of the convenant, nor a radical repudiation of its promise, but rather a tough-minded renegotiating of the covenant on pragmatic, but far from unprincipled, terms.

Hawthorne had his Custom House. Warren had the Library of Congress, where he occupied the Chair of Poetry during the final months of World War II. While it would be hyperbolic to regard Warren's tenure in Washington during 1944-1945 as the decisive pivot-point in his career, it would be equally wrong to

underplay its importance. For one thing, there is the apt symbolism of the naked fact itself. Against the backdrop of unprecedented global carnage, Warren, a necessary noncombatant,
immersed himself in the often obscure records of his nation's
collective past, and the very institution in which he labored
was a kind of monument to Thomas Jefferson and his faith in
the triumph of Reason. (Jefferson had urged the founding of
such a library; as president, he hired the first librarian; and his
private collection of books became the core of its holdings
when most of the original volumes were destroyed or dis-
persed by the British during the War of 1812.) What Warren
found in the frequently arcane items of Americana he exam-
ined in the recesses of the library testified to humankind's
irrationality and propensity for violence. It thus served to
confirm his darkest suspicions about fallen human nature and
the obstacles it placed in the way of a genuine progress. At the
same time, Warren found confirmation of another sort. Virtue
had managed to survive side by side with vice; it was a factor
in the human equation as well. History might be "fate," but "it
might also prove to be redemption."[6]

Before history can be put to use, its nature must be determined and a method for recovering its value must be formulated. Warren's youthful enthusiasm for the reductive
historicism of Henry Thomas Buckle (*Talking* 194) early gave
way to a more skeptical, and respectful, approach to the subtle
ironies of history. As a young writer, he seems to have adopted
almost instinctively an attitude toward the past that was identifiably "modernist" and can be traced to the writings of Eliot
and Pound. Without arguing for a direct influence, James
Longenbach has pointed out the remarkable extent to which
Pound and Eliot's "modernist" (or "existential") mode of historicism had been anticipated by the nineteenth-century the-
orist Wilhelm Dilthey: "When an individual experiences
something in its totality, the relationship ceases to be one of
subject and object; the act of experiencing and the experience
itself become one, and the individual is unified with 'life' itself.
In order to understand the past, consequently, the historian
must breathe his own life into the past, resurrecting the 'lived

experience' of a particular moment in the past through his powers of empathy and intuition. For Dilthey, historical understanding is 'a rediscovery of the I in the thou'; it teaches us not only about the past but about ourselves."[7]

What Longenbach says of Pound and Eliot might be applied with equal justice to Warren: "[They] proceed from the assumption that knowledge does not lie on the surface of events, waiting to be collected by an impartial observer, but lurks within them. To uncover that knowledge, the interpreter must penetrate that surface—and such an effort demands the investment of the interpreter's own experience into his work."[8] As Dilthey himself puts it, "historical insight" is fundamentally an autobiographical act: " 'The power and breadth of our own lives and the energy with which we reflect on them are the foundations of historical vision which enables us to give new life to the bloodless shadows of the past.' "[9]

Longenbach also points to a Crocean correlative to the Diltheyean theorem: " 'every true history is contemporary history.' "[10] The parallel thinking at work in Warren's famous denial that he was a writer of conventional "historical novels," made in the course of an interview with Richard B. Sale in 1969, is apparent: "What I'm trying to find is what happened, something that has the distance of the past but has the image of an issue. It must be an image, a sort of simplified and distant framed image, of an immediate and contemporary issue, a sort of interplay between that image and the contemporary world. That's the only historical novel of interest to me. It must have this personal reference, a feeling of something, whatever that strange thing is that's making that story relevant for you, that involves something that is in you" (*Talking* 128-29). Earlier in his conversation with Sale, Warren had recounted how this same impulse had provided the creative dynamic for *World Enough and Time* (1950), a novel that grew directly out of his reading and meditations in the Library of Congress.

In his first book, *John Brown*, the young Warren had presumed, not altogether rashly, to meditate directly upon an historical moment that was only accessible through formal research. In his first published novel, *Night Rider*, he approached a period that was much more immediately at hand. The Black Patch tobacco wars of the early years of this century were very much a part of the local oral tradition Warren knew during his boyhood, and though he wrote of them with a conscious retrospection, the decades of the 1920s and 1930s, the times depicted in *At Heaven's Gate* and *All the King's Men* respectively, were characterized by a texture of life Warren had experienced firsthand. A rather suggestive pattern emerges here. Moving from biography to fiction, Warren seems, however unconsciously, to have been casting about for a proper subjective stance toward the past, a stance that would reveal most fully the ties between the now and the then he sought to identify and trace.[11] Warren would never deny the factually objective reality of the past, though he would maintain that it could not be ascertained definitively. "The answer is in the back of the book but the page is gone," he wrote in *The Ballad of Billie Potts*,[12] the poem that itself serves, formally and thematically, as a paradigm for the process in question. *Billie Potts* is a dramatic meditation on a *pre*-historical past embodied in legend and myth. Any meaning such meditation may hold is of necessity a product of a mind delimited by the present moment, but the past is no less vital a resource by virtue of that fact. Over and over again in his postwar writing, Warren insisted that a meaningful present and a satisfactory future depend upon a well-formed historical consciousness, a kind of secular equivalent of the Christian's well-formed conscience.

By the mid-1950s, Warren was addressing America's pressing contemporary concerns with a directness unprecedented in his earlier work (even as he increasingly abandoned the pose of Eliotian impersonality in his verse in favor of a more identifiably autobiographical voice), but he did so only after a creative journey into the dark heart of the nation's beginnings where he and his readers confront those "Founders" whose guilt and glory constitute our collective patrimony. Warren's books typically had long gestation periods, and it would be a mistake to oversimplify matters. Still, there is a strong indication that somehow the writing of *World Enough and Time* (1950), *Brother to Dragons* (1953), and (perhaps to a lesser extent) *Band of Angels* (1955) enabled Warren to assume the immediate public stance we find in *Segregation* (1956), *The Legacy of the Civil War* (1961), and *Who Speaks for the Negro?* (1965). It is also telling that, with the notably brilliant exception of *Wilderness* (1961), Warren's later fictions are meditations on the present rather than the past.

The historian/editor who presents us with the narrative of the ill-starred assassin Jeremiah Beaumont in *World Enough and Time* provides the frame of consciousness that enables Warren to connect postwar America with frontier Kentucky in the early nineteenth century, a world that microcosmically mirrors democracy's ongoing struggle to balance off the real and the ideal and wrest from violent disorder a measure of ordered justice.[13] From the outset, the narrator stresses the distance, psychic even more than temporal, that separates yesterday from today. Indeed, though the protagonist's career is unusually well-documented, many of the details surrounding it are little more than "gossip worn thin by a century" or more.[14] Warren's narrator is a scrupulous researcher, but in his conscientious determination to draw firm distinctions between our world and that of Jeremiah Beaumont he frequently goes too far, especially on those occasions when he assumes that Beaumont and his contemporaries were somehow simpler, less complex men and women than their twentieth-century descendants.

The narrator may be right to chastise his modern audience for its own supercilious "self-abasement" and "self-flattery" (*WET* 33)—which are after all but two sides of the same self-indulgent coin—yet it is precisely these two vices that plague Jeremiah Beaumont in the 1820s. The narrator never sufficiently realizes (though he does point out suggestive parallels) just how *contemporary* is his protagonist's plight. That contemporaneity, however, is not lost on the reader if he or she is honest enough to recognize in Beaumont's feckless quest for a separate peace outside the political pressures of his age the roots of an arrogant complacency (born paradoxically of neurosis) hardly unknown in mid-twentieth-century America. Beaumont may conceive of his assassination of Colonel Fort as an act of personal honor, an act of private self-definition, but it is at the same time a political act with horrendous consequences on the body politic. In the end, there may be no truly apolitical acts, for as Warren has remarked elsewhere, in a particularly memorable phrase, "History is what you can't / Resign from."[15]

Yet Beaumont would resign from history. Reading law in Colonel Fort's Bowling Green office, he had once traced mankind's tentative steps "'across the sands of a desert toward some far-off mountain of Justice'" (*WET* 40). His mentor Fort had sought to impress upon him that "'the health of the state is the measure of men's happiness, for if the state was sick that sickness infected all men'" and that therefore "'from whatever intellect and strength a man possessed he should pay tithe and more to the public good'" (*WET* 43). But Beaumont leaves the *law* (literally and figuratively) in a quixotic attempt to restore the ruined "garden" of Rachel Jordan, whose life, she insists, has been blighted by Fort's seduction (yet another private act that proves to have grievious public ramifications). Adam and Eve were expelled from the Garden, leaving all subsequent human generations condemned to work out the history of the race in a fallen world. In presuming to reestablish their own realm of primal innocence, Beaumont and Rachel are in effect seeking to embrace a denatured state that, far from elevating human nature, breeds inhumanity.

More to our purposes here, this same destructive process is embodied throughout the novel in Beaumont's characteristically American dream of achieving a radical redemption in the supposedly untainted stretches of western wilderness. The metaphor of *surveying* (that calling so many Founding Fathers, including Washington himself, pursued in their youth) takes on a crucial significance in this regard. Like his own failed father before him,[16] Beaumont ties his hopes for fulfillment to an activity that in its way aspires to the Godlike task of bringing order out of chaos. To take bearings, make arbitrary measurements, and eventually impose a grid upon previously uncharted territory is an exercise of the mind over recalcitrant matter, an act at once abstractive and artificial. A model in many respects of the Age of Reason's way of coming at the world, surveying in itself changes nothing. Though it is certainly true that Jeremiah Beaumont relates to nature with a pronounced degree of romantic mysticism (with all its overtones of the death wish), his defining approach to the world he inhabits, natural and civil, is finally the reductive way of the surveyor. Again, the act of the mind alone effects no change in nature—particularly in human nature. Whatever rational order the world may come to hold will indeed be a human order, but it must begin with a painfully honest reordering of the individual heart and mind, not in isolation from the public realm, but in recognition of the just claims it exerts over the individual will.

Quite significantly, it is in the "dark entrails of America" (*WET* 418) that Beaumont, seeking to lose himself and Rachel, finds himself at last. For him, as for Dante, the way down, pursued to its utmost extremity, is indeed the way up. Fleeing the justice of the law—the only hope for justice Warren is willing to endorse—Rachel and Beaumont subject themselves to the lawless rule of the monstrous Gran Boz, himself a fugitive from justice on a grander and more grotesque scale. In the heart of the wilderness, the island of Gran Boz is anything but an outpost of civilization. Rather, it is an obscene travesty of the very world, however far from perfect, Beaumont and Rachel have scorned in their adherence to the dictates of an uncompromising ideality.[17] Ironically, the Gran Boz is himself one of the Founding Fathers of modern America. The descendants of his numberless bastards will in time come to vote, pay their taxes, and own "tidy houses with green lawns or subdivision palaces" pursuing useful careers as "farmers, storekeepers, statesmen, heroes, mechanics, insurance agents, executives, bankers" (*WET* 433).

In their scorn of human community, Beaumont and Rachel had immersed themselves in the familiar romantic cult of love and death, yet they ultimately inhabit an underworld where both love and death have been stripped of their value and significance. The Gran Boz fondles Rachel with bored impunity and blandly assures Beaumont that murder is of no consequence. Sexuality and life itself take on meaning only in the context of human community. To step outside that community, to inhabit a counterworld contrived in one's own image, is to descend into the "dark entrails" of the monstrous self; but there *is* meaning, however bitter, in the principle of accountability, and Beaumont's decision to answer the claims of society's justice, to "shake the hangman's hand, and . . . call him brother" (*WET* 460), is a triumph of his agonized wisdom.

The lesson Beaumont learns is a peculiarly American one, encoded in popular narrative forms like the Western and foreshadowed directly in one of the most powerfully realized antecedents of the genre, James Fenimore Cooper's *The Prairie* (1827). In Cooper's Leatherstocking tale, the sociopathic outcast Ishmael Bush, stung by what he perceives as the inherent injustices institutionalized by law, migrates westward away from the restrictions—and the protections—of the legal system. Like Faulkner's character Ab Snopes after him, Ishmael gives precedence to clan loyalty over the pressures of the larger community. In the end, however, he retraces his journey back toward the civilization of the settlements, shattered by his knowledge that the murderous heart of man is no respecter of the ties of kin. Warren's Jeremiah Beaumont must face an even more torturous awakening; he comes to recognize the murderous heart as his own: "that crime for which I seek expiation is never lost. It is always there. It is unpardonable. It is the crime of self, the crime of life. The crime is I" (*WET* 458).

In *Night Rider*, Warren's first novel, Perse Munn may or may not commit suicide of sorts when he makes himself a target for the posse pursuing him. As touched upon briefly in the preceding chapter, that question is open to divergent interpretations. As with Beaumont later, circumstances conspire to teach Munn that the idealist's quest for uncompromising innocence is too frequently a mask for mankind's most destructive urges. Does he choose to expunge "the crime of self" through death? Be that as it may, Beaumont's desire to "shake the hangman's hand" is anything but a simple, suicidal expression of the death wish he has entertained throughout so much of *World Enough and Time*. It testifies to this positive willingness to "clasp" his "guilt" and in doing so embrace self-awareness, "knowledge." This is the necessary first step in the process by which "loneliness becomes communion" and "exile" gives way to repatriation (*WET* 460).

Beaumont's compulsion to render his life on paper, to submit to the resistant medium of language the interplay of the real and ideal, is itself the most dramatic evidence of his striving to *communicate*—in the fullest sense of the word. Warren's narrator notes the aptness of the fact that the final entries in the journal of Jeremiah Beaumont are recorded upon seemingly random sheets of scrap paper (taken from a sermon, a legal document, a land patent, and a map), so that one man's "personal and secret story" is rendered (quite "properly") "on the back of those sheets that document the public and practical life" of an entire people (*WET* 437). Beaumont's candid accounting of his individual past is addressed to the collective present, as the narrator makes clear on the very first page of the book: "He was writing to us" (*WET* 3). Furthermore, his journal ends, quite literally, with a question (reiterated by the historian/narrator) in which the dynamic interrelationship of past, present, and future is implicit, a question that contains within itself a compelling moral imperative: "Was it all for naught?" (*WET* 485). The answer to the question does not reside in the events of the past but in the actions of the present moment as they in turn give rise to the future. The narrator reminds us that *"men still long for justice"* (*WET* 485), even in the midst of postwar complacencies and neuroses. Beaumont's blind errors, misguided ideals, and consequent sufferings are not for naught provided we are prepared to learn from them and carry our new and sobering knowledge into action. This is the burden of Warren's eloquent manifesto of the mid-1950s, "Knowledge and the Image of Man," with its double-edged indictment of New Deal ingenuousness and Eisenhower-era complacency.[18] It is also the basis for Thomas Jefferson's renewed, if torturously chastened, optimism at the conclusion of *Brother to Dragons*, a work in which Warren's particular brand of "dialogic imagination" is given its fullest realization.[19]

I have considered Warren's "tale in verse and voices" at some length elsewhere.[20] Indeed, *Brother to Dragons*, like *All the King's Men*, has attracted a considerable body of critical commentary, much of it of a distinguished nature. But perhaps too little stress has been placed upon the extent to which the work is future-oriented. The brutal lessons that shake Mr. Jefferson's Enlightenment faith in humankind's innate rationality and goodness are convincing enough, but they tell only half the story. The Jeffersonian dream of a nation where liberty and justice are the final goals is invalid only in terms of certain of its initial assumptions and premises. Jefferson had mistakenly sought to design a civil edifice along the lines of the Maison Quarée at Nîmes, a structure informed by "the eternal / Light of just proportion and the heart's harmony."[21] But it is the precariously balanced dynamism of Gothic architecture, in which dream and nightmare, hope and fear mesh, that provides a more fitting and workable metaphor for the American republic.

At Philadelphia, drafting the Declaration, Jefferson had looked toward a future cleansed of the nightmare past, an unsullied new beginning; by the end of *Brother to Dragons*, he is ready to renegotiate the democratic covenant on a more realistic and realizable basis: "the dream of the future is not / Better than the fact of the past, no matter how terrible. / For without the fact of the past we cannot dream the future" (*BD* 193). Undeniably, the future we dream carries with it an awesome price: "It will be forged beneath the hammer of truth / On the anvil of our anguish." Nonetheless, the promise of history resides in that ongoing process through which we turn today into tomorrow and in doing so reshape and define ourselves through action and commitment:

> . . . if there is to be reason, we must
> Create the possibility
> Of reason, and we can create it only
> From the circumstances of our most evil despair.
> We must strike the steel of wrath on the stone of guilt,
> And hope to provoke, thus, in the midst of our coiling darkness
> The incandescence of the heart's great flare.

And in that illumination I should hope to see
How all creation validates itself,
For whatever you create, you create yourself by it,
And in creating yourself you will create
The whole wide world and gleaming West anew. [*BD* 194-95]

Thus speaks the Jefferson of *Brother to Dragons*, and Warren's persona, R.P.W.,[22] provides a summary codicil to Jefferson's words several pages later: "If there is glory, the burden, then, is ours. / If there is virtue, the burden, then, is ours" (*BD* 211). We should not lose sight of the fact that the "present" of *Brother to Dragons* centers upon the Korean War and the domestic boom that accompanied it (a fact pointedly alluded to in crucial passages in the text). It is this ambiguous "world of action and liability" (*BD* 215) that R.P.W. himself reenters at the work's conclusion, a world paradoxically rendered "Sweeter than hope" by the poet's new sense, at once restrained and exhilarating, of America's possibilities. America may indeed be "great Canaan's grander counterfeit" (*BD* 11), at one level a fraudulent secular substitute for the biblical Promised Land. But in another sense, it embodies a "grander" promise, provided we pursue the twin burdens of "glory" and "virtue" with the humility our history, properly assimilated, teaches us.

Warren submits that we owe as much to those "Founders," whether famous, infamous, or simply forgotten, who gave us the burden and promise of our moment in time. They could provide their descendants no absolute answers to the quandaries of the second half of the twentieth century, but they did bequeath to them a new world, however problematic. Their lives might be accessible only through a historicism of the imagination, but we are obliged to maintain our tenuous lines of communication with them nonetheless. Warren put it this way in "Founding Fathers, Nineteenth-Century Style, Southeast U.S.A.":

> . . . they died, and are dead, and now their voices
Come thin, like the last cricket in frost-dark, in grass lost,
With nothing to tell us for our complexity of choices,
But beg us only one word to justify their own old life-cost.

So let us bend ear to them in this hour of lateness,
And what they are trying to say, try to understand,
And try to forgive them their defects, even their greatness,
For we are their children in the light of humanness, and under the
    shadow of God's closing hand.[23]

In another poem from *Promises* (1957), "Infant Boy at Mid-century," Warren would ask that his son's generation accord his own a similar measure of pious consideration: "Remember our defects, we give them to you gratis. / But remember that ours is not the worst of times" (52). The middle of the twentieth century might be an age in which Americans suffered from private unease even in the midst of public professions of national confidence ("the neurotic clock-tick / Of midnight competes with the heart's pulsed assurance of power" [48]), but like all periods in history it offered the possibility for virtue, private and public. The Supreme Court's decision in the case of *Brown v. The Board of Education*, which opened the floodgates for a revolution in civil rights, confronted the nation with a dramatic test of its capacity for courage and virtue, and the unique occasion this presented for a renewal and reinvigoration of the American covenant was not lost on Robert Penn Warren.

America's situation in the wake of *Brown v. The Board of Education* resembled in certain pointed ways the circumstances facing the character Tobias Sears at the end of Warren's *Band of Angels*. Tobias, the idealistic son of a wealthy New Englander who is at once a personal friend of Emerson and a precursor of the Gilded Age moguls, fights in the Civil War to free the slaves and works subsequently with the Freedmen's Bureau, but later events, culminating in the "Great Betrayal" of 1877, combine to leave him cynical on the race question. Wedded for better or worse to Amantha Starr, whose own parentage (her father a white planter, her mother a slave) makes her a living emblem of the American South, Tobias gradually drifts westward, reenacting the perennial New World pattern of new beginnings and disappointed hopes. At the book's conclusion, however, he undergoes a more substantial kind of rebirth. However reluctantly, Tobias finds himself taking up again the black man's cause. Indeed, his self-respect demands that he do so. He comes to realize that white and black alike share a common destiny, and he finds that the quest for justice is enlivening, if hazardous.

The failure of Reconstruction and the decades of "separate-but-equal" that followed meant that the dream of racial justice had long been deferred in America, that finding a fuller place for blacks within the American experiment remained a nagging unfinished business. By the mid-1950s, the old complacencies, hypocrisies, and fatalistic sense of resignation were no longer viable. A genuine crusade of sorts was underway, and Warren returned to the South to witness the turmoil firsthand. Segregation was by no means a purely southern "problem"; it could only be eradicated through a determined exertion of the national will.[24] But southern communities were the principal scenes against which this historical drama was being played out with the greatest emotional intensity. Accordingly, Warren, the self-exiled southerner living in suburban Connecticut, traveled south to gauge the fears and hopes of southerners of both races and various castes.

What he learned he distilled into a compact but powerful book, *Segregation*. In the "Author's Note" at the outset, Warren described this volume with deceptive simplicity as *"a report of conversations, some of which had been sought out and some of which came as the result of chance encounters."*[25] In reality, these disparate "conversations" act contrapuntally to form a single testament, not unlike the often wrangling "voices" that convey the total vision of *Brother to Dragons*. Warren, assuming the role of interlocutor, was determined to move beyond the clichés of "fear" and "hate" that dominated the journalism of the period. The voices in *Segregation* testify to a profound "self-division" in the psyche of the South—and in the larger social fabric of America itself. By the book's end, Warren makes it clear that it is an act of bad faith to assume that we must reconcile ourselves to the status of "prisoners of our history" (*Segregation* 62). To do so is to invest unwisely in a version of the Great Alibi he would take pains to undermine in

a later book, *The Legacy of the Civil War*. In his preface to
Brother to Dragons, Warren had already stated firmly his conviction that, while we might be compelled to live the *myth* that
is history, we can, by virtue of our moral volition, reshape and
"remake" that destiny we at once struggle against and labor
toward. The integration of both society and the self depend
upon it.

Yet Warren recognized, even in himself, the false sense of
"relief" that forever tempts men and women to take flight from
"responsibility" (*Segregation* 51). Winging his way north out of
Memphis, he thinks:

Now you may eat the bread of the Pharisee and read in the morning
paper, with only a trace of irony, how out of an ultimate misery of
rejection some Puerto Rican school boys—or is it Jews or Negroes or
Italians?—who call themselves something grand, The Red Eagles or
the Silver Avengers, have stabbed another boy to death, or raped a
girl, or trampled an old man into a bloody mire. If you can afford it,
you will, according to the local mores, send your child to a private
school, where there will be, of course, a couple of Negro children on
exhibit. And that delightful little Chinese girl who is so good at
dramatics. Or is it finger painting? [*Segregation* 51-52]

Such a bogus "relief" is, Warren knows, a self-deceptive denial
of "the reality you were born to," and *Segregation* ends with
Warren conducting one final interview—"an interview with
myself"—in which he states without equivocation that "we
have to deal with the problem our historical moment proposes,
the burden of our time" (*Segregation* 65). To do less is to deny
ourselves. Racial justice, Warren makes plain, will not come
quickly ("Gradualism is all you'll get." [*Segregation* 65]), but
here too historical perspective is important: "desegregation is
just one small episode in the long effort for justice. It seems to
me that that perspective, suddenly seeing the business as little,
is a liberating one. It liberates you from yourself" (*Segregation*
64). Unlike the flight from responsibility, *this* self-liberation is
tied to a resolute engagement with the burdens of "our historical moment."

Were evidence of the ironies of American history required at
this point, it is only necessary to remember that the height of

the civil rights struggle intersected in a most suggestive and symbolically charged manner with America's commemoration of a literal Civil War that had radically changed the direction of the national life a century before. Warren's newly intensified concern with what the popular press dubbed the "Negro Revolution" and his long-standing fascination with the War Between the States came together with serendipitous results in both *Wilderness* and *The Legacy of the Civil War*. (The latter also contained some cautionary insights into the causes and potential costs, military and moral, of the ongoing Cold War.)[26] But it is the documentary *Who Speaks for the Negro?* that stands as Warren's most direct and most fully realized witness to his age. In its pages, the substance of his prophetic vision is virtually ubiquitous, but that vision is never imposed upon events or conversations. Rather, it is allowed to manifest itself dynamically in terms of a compelling inner logic.

Of the myriad black voices that speak in response to Warren's probing questions, three stand out as particularly significant—those of Dr. Martin Luther King, Jr., Malcolm X, and Ralph Ellison. The first two are avowedly religious visionaries and would become martyrs. Indeed, they may be regarded as alternate sides of the same coin, avatars of a deep split in the religious sensibility of mankind, not merely in the attitudes of Afro-Americans. In Ralph Ellison, Warren presents his reader with another kind of visionary, an artist whose art is inescapably tied to the fact of his marginal racial status but who refuses to subordinate the rich complexity of his personal experience to the demands of any single social agenda. As in *Segregation*, it is Warren who is the unspoken protagonist of *Who Speaks for the Negro?*,[27] and his quest for understanding is revealed unmistakably as he defines himself in relation to these three black Americans. (To be sure, King and Malcolm, in terms of their personalities and the general outlines of their careers, bear uncanny similarities with certain characters out of Warren's novels, and Ellison stands as a kind of alter ego to Warren himself.)

Warren is clearly struck by the way in which historical circumstances served to thrust Martin Luther King, Jr., into a position of leadership. The Montgomery bus boycott brought King into a low-key and unspectacular degree of direct involvement in the burgeoning protests against segregation, but it was only when his own house was bombed and he articulated his radical commitment to nonviolence as a tool for achieving social justice that King leaped to prominence and demonstrated an awareness of the responsibilities leadership entailed. Dr. King's repudiation of violence, even in a just cause, as ultimately self-destructive is akin to that of Captain Todd in *Night Rider*, and like Colonel Fort in *World Enough and Time* he knows that the complexity of historical events and human personalities work against absolute solutions to moral questions, calling instead for a spirit of compromise.

Warren poses to King the suggestion of Gunnar Myrdal that financial compensation to the slaveholders after Emancipation might have served to mitigate the course of racial relations in the South, and King, without for a moment supposing that slavery was anything but an indefensible evil, responds that the period following the Civil War was indeed "tragic" because of its missed opportunities. The well-intentioned engineers of Reconstruction had lacked foresight in part because they had failed to respect the density of historical precedent: "after two hundred and forty-four years of slavery, certain patterns had developed in the minds of people, so everybody had to take some form of responsibility. Consequently in solving the problem it seems to me maybe some things would have had to be done which may not have represented everything that we would want to see. But it might have saved us many of the bitter moments we now have."[28] Implicitly, King faults the single-minded idealists who denied the human and historical vagaries that accompany all historical change. Slavery had presented the nation with an "accumulated . . . social problem that had to be grappled with" (*WSN* 213). Because easy answers were applied to complex questions, the grappling had been unnecessarily intensified and prolonged. (Compare this to Warren's remark later in *Who Speaks for the Negro?* that the Civil War itself—"the shock treatment of 1861-65"—provided "only the illusion of a cure" to the deep dissociations of the

1850s that came to be conveniently focussed around the issue of slavery [321].) Leaving aside the question of how far Warren goes in redrawing King in accordance with his writerly predispositions, his reaction to King's response to Myrdal's hypothesis is most significant: "I remember his face. . . . He no longer seemed aware of my presence. His face was drawing together, sharpening inwardly, his eyes seemed veiled. There was some tension, as far as I could determine. But he was not the kind of man to deny one pole of the question. He was sitting there, aware of both, living through the question. Perhaps that is the deepest kind of life he knows. His philosophy is a way of living with an intense polarity" (*WSN* 213).

Somewhat later, Warren notes how King's voice, when taking up the kind of question that engages him at the deepest level, assumes "a balanced rhythm, a long movement up, then a sharper fall away, the movement balanced by another like it, pair by pair." At first, this strikes Warren as an artificial resorting to platform oratory, but he revises this hypothesis, suggesting instead that perhaps the "deep balance of rhythm had some relation to the attempt to deal with and include antitheses, to affirm and absorb the polarities of life" (*WSN* 221). Warren does not make the connection explicitly, but he clearly presents King's meditative responses as analogous to that "impure," irony-driven poetry he called for in his critical essays of the 1940s and sought to approximate in his own writing, in particular when it came to dealing with that "complex fate" Henry James identified as the peculiar legacy of the American.

If Warren approves of, and identifies with, Martin Luther King's acknowledgment of the world's tensions and the irreducibility of history's paradoxes, the same cannot be said for his attitude toward Malcolm X. Malcolm's adherence to what Warren portrays as the racist absurdities of the Black Muslim religion, his insinuative flirtation with violence, and his instinct for linking self-promotion with the furtherance of his cause are clearly repugnant to Warren, at least on the surface. Nevertheless, Malcolm fascinates Warren more than repels him, for he, like John Brown and Jeremiah Beaumont, is more complicated than his public role will allow. Warren obviously

senses things about this troubled and troubling black visionary that will only be fully verified when Alex Haley brings out
The Autobiography of Malcolm X following Malcolm's assassination.[29] Yet already, Warren sees in the almost archetypal pattern of Malcolm's career the dramatic makings of a
modern hero.

A child whose early life was marred by violence and poverty,
a bright student nevertheless marginalized by his race, an
amoral hustler wise to the ways of the street, a prisoner who
undergoes a radical religious transformation, a constant
"thorn in the side" of complacent white America—in each of
the stages of his self-evolution, Malcolm X had proven himself
to be (even though Warren detects in him a decided measure of
the histrionic) an inveterate "seeker, a quester" (*WSN* 264). In
a memorable passage, Warren reads Malcolm as symbol:
"Malcolm X is many things. He is the face not seen in the
mirror. He is the threat not spoken. He is the nightmare self. He
is the secret sharer" (*WSN* 266). But Warren had already made
it emphatically clear that Malcolm X was first and last a most
elusive human being, impossible to relegate to simple stereo-
type *or* psychological symbol: "he is a man of great talents and
great personal magnetism. He knows that psychologists, and
not philosophers, rule the world. He is, like all men of power, a
flirt, he flirts with destiny. He conceives of the general situation as fluid and he has made his own situation fluid. He is free
to tack, to play the wind. He trusts his magnetism—and his
luck. He may end at the barricades. Or in Congress. Or he
might even end on the board of a bank" (*WSN* 264). Instead,
Malcolm went to Mecca, where he would seem to have found
the ultimate object of his lifelong quest in an Islam that
preached the value of an integrated self functioning within a
human community that transcended the boundaries of race.
Like Warren's Willie Stark, he was headed home at last. *Who
Speaks for the Negro?* was in press at the time of Malcolm's
death in February 1965, but Warren hastened to add a final
word on this man who, in his assessment, "had something of
the scale of personality and force of will we associate with the
tragic hero" (*WSN* 267).[30]

It is Ralph Ellison, the author of *Invisible Man* (1952), one of the most distinguished of modern American novels, who stands out as the real "secret sharer" of Warren's vision. Warren handles the more militant James Baldwin with a respectful, but pointedly skeptical, degree of empathy as a fellow artist, but in Ellison he recognizes a fully kindred spirit. If Baldwin in his anger emerges as the literary equivalent of a Malcolm X, Ellison possesses the inwardness and self-authenticity Warren admired in Dr. King. In the course of his conversation with Warren, Ellison reveals himself as an enemy of abstractions. Only too painfully aware through his own varied experience of the dehumanizing tendencies of institutions, Ellison nonetheless shares with Warren a sense of the inescapability of a universal *human* condition all men and women partake of, apart from the particulars of time and place. He thus finds fault with the assertation of Le Roi Jones (Imamu Amiri Baraka) that the slave "'cannot be a man.'" Ellison, quite characteristically, frames his response to such a notion in the form of a question: "isn't it closer to the truth that far from considering themselves only in terms of that abstraction, 'a slave,' the enslaved really thought of themselves as *men* who had been unjustly enslaved?" (*WSN* 331).

Without underplaying the special burden slavery and segregation placed upon black Americans, Ellison can see that the white middle class, especially its youth, also suffers at this moment in history from a version of cultural deprivation, an impoverishment of purpose and identity tied up with a loss of the sense of the past. Ellison might almost be speaking for Warren when he says, "I think there's a terrific crisis [among white Americans], and one of the events by which the middle class is being tested, and one of the forms in which the crisis expresses itself is the necessity of dealing with the Negro freedom movement" (*WSN* 338). Ellison conceives of the civil rights struggle in terms that speak to Warren's own sense of the struggle's mutual importance to both races when he insists on seeing it primarily as an attempt "to bring America's conduct into line with its professed ideals" (*WSN* 339). The "moment of historical truth" (*WSN* 340) had at last caught up with Americans, black and white, and Ellison's prescription for meeting the moment might almost have come from the mouth of Warren himself. Addressing himself to the challenge of facing ourselves, Ellison says: "This places a big moral strain upon the individual, and it requires self-confidence, self-consciousness, self-mastery, insight, and compassion. In the broader sense it requires an alertness to human complexity. Men in our situation simply cannot afford to ignore the nuances of human relationships. And although action is necessary, forthright action, it must be guided—tempered by insight and compassion" (*WSN* 343).

How can such "insight and compassion," the necessary prerequisites for lasting social reform, be acquired? How can the self-integration essential to a revisioning of the Founders' dream be achieved? One important way is through the prophetic practice of the writer's craft that at its highest level combines (in Warren's words) "the moral effort to see and recognize the truth of the self and the world" with "the artistic effort to say the truth" (*WSN* 347). Warren praises Ellison as just such a writer, one who knows that "if 'truth' moves into 'art,' so 'art' can move backward (and forward) into 'truth'" (*WSN* 348). Literature not only partakes of the world, it addresses the world, and for this reason it had best resist the easy security of a presumptive ideology.

Ellison argues that a circumscribed vision yields inferior art, and his objection to such productions is by no means purely aesthetic: "bad art which toys with serious issues is ultimately destructive and the entertainment which it provides is poisonous" (*WSN* 334). Warren is in full agreement.[31] In an America in which even the children of the most privileged classes suffer from what Bayard Rustin termed a "poverty of plenty" (*WSN* 243) arising from psychic rootlessness and a concomitant lack of selfhood, the responsibilities of the literary artist are more pressing than ever before. For Warren and Ellison, more than racial justice was at stake in the turbulent 1960s; the future of American democracy, grounded on the *integrity* of the individual, was in the balance. Warren had made his awareness of the systemic crisis facing the nation

explicit in the course of an encomium to the black activist
Whitney Young: "He [Young] is attacking, instinctively perhaps, the great dehumanizing force of our society: the fragmentation of the individual through the fragmentation of
function and the draining away of opportunity for significant
moral responsibility—the fragmentation of community
through the fragmentation of the individual" (*WSN* 171).

In a nation rapidly assuming the characteristics of vacuity
and facelessness, literature, "returning us to the world and to
ourselves," offered a vestigial source of hope, since it not only,
in Warren's words, "reconciles us with reality" but "helps us
deal with reality."[32] One way to get at the heart of Warren's
fiction and poetry from the mid-1950s on is to regard it as a
sustained attack upon unreality's usurpation of the real.

At opposite ends of the political spectrum, Bogan Murdock in
At Heaven's Gate and Willie Stark in *All the King's Men* were
both portrayed by Warren as enemies of the democratic covenant, and it is no accident that they shared an important
talent: a gift for packaging themselves and their respective
agendas in most seductive terms. Both were masters in manipulating the power of the image. The tools available to a
Murdock in the 1920s and a Stark in the 1930s were limited,
however, in comparison with the advances in electronic communication that proliferated in the wake of the Second World
War. What the historian Daniel Boorstin described as the long-
standing Graphic Revolution had become an ever-accelerating
process, open to sinister manipulation by power brokers to be
sure, but even more to be feared by virtue of its inherent
tendency to supplant the actual with the illusory. In his now-
classic *The Image, or What Happened to the American Dream*
(1962), Boorstin set about to "describe the world of our making,
how we have used our wealth, our literacy, our technology, and
our progress, to create the thicket of unreality which stands
between us and the facts of life." "I [will] recount," Boorstin
promised his reader, the "historical forces which have given us
this unprecedented opportunity to deceive ourselves and to
befog our experience."[33]

By the 1960s, Boorstin submitted, "The making of the illusions which flood our experience has become the business
of America" (*Image* 5). Surveying the malaise besetting the
United States in the second half of the twentieth century, Boorstin further asserted, "What ails us most is not what we have
done with America, but what we have substituted for America"
(*Image* 6). According to Boorstin, the seductive power of false
"images" resides in humankind's instinctive recoil from the
harshness of the human predicament, with its intimidating
array of complexities; the bogus "image" at once panders to
our thirst for the extraordinary and to our desire for an easy
cure to our existential uneasiness. "There is no cure," Boorstin
says at his book's conclusion: "There is only the opportunity for
discovery. For this the New World gave us a grand, unique
beginning" (*Image* 261). If the American experiment, the bright
and enabling *dream*, is to regain its viability, Americans must
"discover anew where dreams end and where illusions begin"
(*Image* 261).

Boorstin's *The Image* may be said to constitute an uninten-
tional gloss on Warren's *The Cave* (1959). The denizens of Plato's
allegorical cave were epistemological prisoners of their senses,
mistaking the flitting shadows projected upon the wall opposite them for the realities of the Ideal.[34] In *The Cave*, Warren
reverses this symbol, showing how the "ideal" images generated by Big Media, the incestuous realm of advertising, popular entertainment, and electronic communications, subvert
the immediacy of the phenomenological world and serve to
eviscerate human experience. Rather than accept the vulnera-
bility of his problematic identity, the Greek cafe-owner Nick
Pappy seeks confirmation of selfhood in consumer-culture
props like brand-name bourbon and a flashy automobile. Until
he undergoes a chastening of sorts, he can only love his wife by
fantasizing her into the role of Jean Harlow. In similar fashion,
the banker Timothy Bingham is only able to visualize the
future happiness of his daughter in terms of a full-color adver-
tisement in a slick magazine: "He could not understand why
the thought of the picture of them—Jo-Lea, Monty, and the
baby—should be even sweeter than the thought of them as

real." The answer presents itself: "The picture, he guessed, was more outside some of the trouble of life."[35] Indeed, it represents a denial of life.

The Cave relentlessly follows the process through which one family's personal tragedy is abstracted and depersonalized. It documents how communal solidarity is transformed into what Boorstin would call a "pseudo-event," packaged for popular consumption with an eye toward financial profit. The chief perverter of reality in the novel is Isaac (Little Ikey) Sumpter. Erroneously assumed by many to be a Jew, Isaac is Warren's sardonic portrait of the new chosen one, the New World man who would inherit the counterfeit Canaan of American success, a land not of milk and honey but of scotch, Seconal, and loveless sexuality. Destined to become a big shot in Big Media, Isaac will orchestrate the plight of Jasper Harrick, trapped in a Kentucky cave, into the materials of a full-fledged media blitz in which wire services, radio, and television compete with one another to supply the details of Jasper's ordeal (many of them manufactured whole cloth) to a jaded public made up of eager and sensation-starved consumers.

In contrast, Jasper's brother Monty composes a heartfelt, if somewhat inept, ballad that, in its simple directness, affirms the essential human dimension of the buried man's fate. Likewise, the members of the immediate community gather on the mountainside to express their support of the Harrick family through prayer and hymns. But they are soon joined by thrill-seeking outsiders and, in frenzied response to media hysteria, the gathering ends with a plunge into Dionysian oblivion—Warren's reminder of the dark forces that technology cannot dispel and may even serve to unleash. Isaac Sumpter reaps his reward. In the plush executive offices of a major network, he will at last occupy his version of the Promised Land, ironically a place of exile and quiet desperation, the "counterfeit" Canaan. This purveyor of the insubstantial must live with the knowledge of his own insubstantiality.

One of the climactic scenes in *The Cave* might almost be regarded as emblematic of its author's intentions in writing the novel. When Mrs. Harrick finally realizes the hopelessness of her son's situation, she cries out with uncontrollable grief, which makes her an ideal subject upon which to concentrate the full glare of media attention. Nick Pappy realizes in a way he cannot quite articulate that the "powerful light" of the camera and intrusive presence of the microphone represent a profanation and debasement of the moment: "He had plunged toward the guys with the mike things. He had shoved them aside. He had shoved the camera back. He was yelling: 'Leave her alone!'"[36] Warren, in writing *The Cave*, is engaged in a similar action, and his book is at once a striking out against the media's meretricious demeaning of the human condition and a determined effort to restore and record the fully human on its own terms.

Brad Tolliver and Yasha Jones in *Flood* (1964) yearn to achieve a similar reclamation of the human dimension through art when they converge on the doomed community of Fiddlersburg, Tennessee, soon to be inundated by the waters that will feed a hydroelectrical plant, a triumph of technological progress that promises to brighten a supposedly benighted region with unlimited *artificial* light. Two illusion-merchants from the fantasy kingdom of Hollywood, where they have instinctively drifted in flight from their pasts and themselves, Brad and Yasha may well be commendable in their quest to recapture what was real about a given American time and place, but their efforts prove in vain. The America of false façades, of tinseled glamour, of fairy-tale self-deceptions— an America Brad and Yasha have had a hand in making—has already buried all but the last vestigial remnants of the America that was, a world that now seems only available through a nostalgic and sentimentalizing reverie. Yet Fiddlersburg had never been an idyllic place, as Brad Tolliver has reason enough to know from his boyhood there, and to look back upon it with a naive longing is merely to surrender to the same demand for illusion to which the Hollywood and television image-makers pander. Again, for Warren there had never been time in history when the stark realities of human life were not a constant. Living with ourselves had always been humankind's most distressing challenge, though the sense of selfhood might indeed be under unprecedented assault in the brave new world of the present media moment. In the very act of writing *Flood*, Warren was expressing his faith that the literary imagination could, if exercised with an uncompromising determination to reveal the ironic complexities of human experience, restore the sense of self—in all its contingency. *Flood* presumes to present its readers with the unsettling, but ultimately liberating, "truth" about the underlying phenomenological world of ambiguities and paradoxes they are destined—and privileged—to inhabit.

While Warren, as a *literary* man, quite naturally looked upon the writing of fiction and poems as a counterforce to the abstractive threat of the mass media, others, most notably Marshall McLuhan, celebrated the communications revolution as an "extension" of the human, even as they recognized the profound anxiety that accompanies any rapid advance in technologies. A Catholic, and fundamentally a man of the most conservative instincts committed to what he saw as the possibility of regaining the wholeness of the world and the self, McLuhan had once been attracted to the ideology of the former Agrarians.[37] Yet in *Understanding Media: The Extensions of Man*, one of the seminal books of the 1960s, McLuhan implicitly broke ranks with Ransom, Tate, Brooks, and Warren, arguing that the technology of print and the culture of literacy were themselves responsible for the Western mind's disengagement with the world and that the potential for a "global village" arising from communications networking promoted an almost "tribal" reintegration of the alienated individual into the community of the human race. In retrospect, McLuhan's optimism (though one should not dismiss it as wholly unfounded, especially in light of the role media have played in reshaping the political structure of eastern Europe in recent years) may seem altogether too ingenuous. Though Warren declined to answer the specific arguments of McLuhan in detail, he clearly distrusted such theorizing as yet another species of mystified millennialism.[38] Warren too might yearn for the establishment of communion, a recommitment of the alienated individual to a place within the broader social context, but throughout his career he assumed that meaningful community could only be made up of fully individuated selves. *Self*-knowledge was a precondition for responsible commitment to the social realm, and that presupposed a "separateness" that had to be acknowledged and embraced.[39] Even love depends upon loneliness, as Warren demonstrated most compellingly in *Meet Me in the Green Glen* (1971).[40]

McLuhan was no doubt right in seeing the print revolution as a fracturing of older, ostensibly more "organic," modes of communal experience, but the spread of literacy, it should be remembered, corresponded hand-in-glove with the evolution of those nascent democratic social theories aimed at reconciling the just demands of the newly particularized, post-Cartesian self with the traditional prerogatives of the greater community. Whatever technetronic order McLuhan may have imagined would clearly be less radically individualistic than the polis envisioned by Founders like Jefferson, who sought to erect their new order squarely upon the freedom of the press, thus declaring their trust in the centrality of the readerly/ writerly vocation to the realization of self within society. Nowhere was Warren's preference for the problematics of democracy over the specious promises of all utopianisms more manifest than in his insistence upon the importance of literature as an exploration and assertion of selfhood, and nowhere did he address this question with more eloquence and prophetic urgency than in *Democracy and Poetry*, the revised text of the Jefferson Lectures he delivered in 1974, and a book that bears a telling epigraph from St.-John Perse: "it is enough for the poet to be the guilty conscience of his time."

In a schizoid age when Americans appeared to suffer simultaneously from what Arthur M. Schlesinger, Jr., termed a "crisis of confidence" and from a leaden somnambulism Boorstin and others blamed on commercial image-makers,[41] imaginative literature had a vital, and two-fold, role to play. It was, Warren insisted, a potentially powerful ally of the embattled democratic experiment by virtue of its *diagnostic* and *therapeutic* functions. Historically, "our poetry, in fulfilling its function of bringing us face to face with our nature and our fate, has told us, directly or indirectly, consciously or unconsciously, that we are driving toward the destruction of the very assumption on which our nation is presumably founded."[42] The Founders had aimed at nurturing "the free man, the responsible self" (*DP* 31), but our canonical writers, from Cooper through Dreiser to Faulkner, had documented something quite different: the steady effacement of individual identity and the disintegration of the *self*, which Warren defines as "a moral identity, recognizing itself as capable of action worthy of praise or blame" (*DP* xiii). America's writers were the authors of the nation's inner history, chroniclers of the degree to which professed ideals had fallen short of realization. As such, they were diagnosticians of the first order, but their role, Warren argued, was by no means finished. Their record of all-too-human weaknesses could itself become a potential source of strength—for each self-as-citizen and, by extension, for a deeply troubled nation at large. If "the long drift of our American civilization has been *toward* the abolition of the self" (*DP* 68), "poetry"—by which Warren meant the work of the literary imagination in the broadest sense—serves to subvert by its very nature such a process. The poem or novel is at once an embodiment and an affirmation of selfhood: "The 'made thing' becomes . . . a vital emblem of the struggle toward the achieving of the self, and the mark of that struggle, the human signature, is what gives the aesthetic organization its numinousness" (*DP* 69). The creation of a work entails "a plunge into the 'abyss of the self,' " and the engaged reader is induced to take a similar plunge, "to explore the possibilities of his own 'abyss.' "[43] In this way, literature "wakes us up to our own life" (*DP* 71). It may, Warren proceeds to suggest, do more. It may trigger the energy necessary to effect a change, in ourselves and in the world in which we live. Poetry might thus serve to renew the democratic impulse, even in post-Vietnam, post-Watergate America.

Throughout *Democracy and Poetry*, Warren describes the work of literature as an "adventure in selfhood." That phrase might be productively applied to the entire sweep of his career, and more particularly to his sustained poetic output in the last two decades of his life. In five volumes of new verse, ranging from *Incarnations* (1968) to *Rumor Verified* (1981), Warren labored, almost compulsively it seemed, to explore and express his personal memories, fears, and joys. Often private, but never "confessional" in the manner of a Robert Lowell, these poems are not infrequently examples of what MacLeish would call "public speech," manifestations of a specifically American experience, a poetry rife with potential consequences. Warren would assume the prophet's mantle even more fully and directly in three remarkable long poems: *Audubon* (1969), *Chief Joseph of the Nez Perce* (1983), and "New Dawn" (included in the summational *New and Selected Poems* of 1985).

Audubon, the transplanted European of ambiguous origins who undergoes a nearly fatal ordeal in the depths of the American wilderness and then emerges with a renewed commitment to making his vision a manifest reality, is Warren's portrait of the artist confronting his fate in the New World,[44] and the poem that bears his name stands as an implicit disquisition on the marginality of the artist in American commercial society even as it insists upon the communal value of the artistic enterprise in and of itself. Audubon takes as his subject a nature that is as brutal and predatory as it is beautiful; his is an art of confrontation, not evasion. It represents finally an affirmation, but an affirmation that can only come about through an immersion in hardship, self-denial, and violence. The clear relationship between Audubon, the painter of birds, and Warren, the maker of verses, points toward the poet's insistence throughout his later writings that *made-things* are somehow necessary, especially at our point in history:

> Tell me a story.
>
> In this century, and moment, of mania,
> Tell me a story.
>
> Make it a story of great distance, and starlight.
>
> The name of the story will be Time,
> But you must not pronounce its name.
>
> Tell me a story of deep delight.[45]

The necessary fiction, for Warren, does not begin (as Robert Frost would have it) in delight and end in wisdom; the wisdom must be earned first. The consequent "delight" is "deep" because it originates *de profundis*.

Yet another such paradoxical "story of deep delight" is *Chief Joseph*, published some dozen years after *Audubon* and born out of the depths of America's shameful history of double-dealing with its indigenous peoples. Warren's account of the Nez Perce War, a brilliantly polyphonic example of its author's characteristic dialogism, is in many ways the closest thing to an epic Warren ever wrote. Indeed, it would seem to have pleased the poet Robert Fitzgerald, the masterful translator of Homer and Virgil.[46] Warren sets for himself the task of reclaiming (through an imagination fully aware of its own limitations) whatever "truth" history (approached with a realist's skeptical reverence) may deign to yield. The white officials who lie to Joseph and his band in a very real sense lie to themselves, and what passes for history, Warren warns us, is itself too often a lie, a travesty of the hard human costs of the past. Buffalo Bill, as Warren depicts him, stands for the American impulse to domesticate the tragic processes of history by reducing them to self-flattering images of melodramatic conflict. Anticipating the image-makers of the present day, the inventor of the Wild West show was a "magician who could transform / For howling patriots, or royalty, / The blood of history into red ketchup, / A favorite American condiment."[47] An analogy may be in order: if too much of what passes for our national past is pure image, Warren in *Chief Joseph* aspires to represent a portion of our collective legacy in an iconographic way, investing his reclamation of the past with that numinous dimension he called for in *Democracy and Poetry*. But the confrontation with the past is not an end in itself for Warren or his reader, and the poem's final section makes it clear that the writer's ultimate concern is with his nation's shaky present and even more problematic future.

In "New Dawn," Warren turned his attention to a development that had served to render the future of America, and indeed of the human race as a whole, more problematic than ever before—the birth of the Atomic Age. Nearly four decades after the fact, Warren recreated in a terse poem of fifteen sections the dropping of the Bomb on Hiroshima, and whereas he had introduced himself explicitly at the conclusion of both *Audubon* and *Chief Joseph*, in "New Dawn" he is present only by virtue of his disembodied narrative voice. The effect is all the more chilling. As in his early short fiction, the events here largely speak on their own terms, though Warren cannot resist from time to time the dark sardonic irony that had been one of his trademarks from *John Brown* on:

> Weather reports good from spotters.
> Three options: Nagasaki, Kokura, Hiroshima.
>
> But the message of one spotter:
> "Advise bombing primary"—i.e.,
> Hiroshima.
>
> Already preferred by Tibbets.
>
> What added satisfaction it would have been to know that
> At 7:31 A.M. Japanese Time, the
> All Clear signal sounds over Hiroshima.[48]

Colonel Tibbets and the crew of the *Enola Gay* (code-named "Dimples") are not hardened killers, but rather happy—indeed boyish—warriors who play the deadly game of war with a kind of innocent enthusiasm: "just don't / Screw it up. Let's do this really great!"[49] Unlike John Hersey,[50] whose classic work of reportage *Hiroshima* (1946; rev. 1985) records the horrors unleashed upon the civilians of the Japanese city in the wake of the *Enola Gay*'s mission, Warren focusses upon the American airmen almost exclusively, implying that they too, whether they face the fact or not, are secondary victims of an act of technological savagery that forever changed the course of civilization. Having triggered the release of a new age of unprecedented potential for destructiveness, they return to Tinian Island to a hero's welcome. Representatives of the best and brightest young men of their generation, they bring with them a moral fallout that continues to inflict their nation and the world, troubling all subsequent dreams of the future. "New Dawn" is "public speech" of the most compelling kind.

Audubon, Chief Joseph of the Nez Perce, and "New Dawn" are to varying degrees *frontier* poems. As such, they serve as reminders that Warren always tended to envision the American experience in terms of boundaries and borders. Straddling the frequently vague line of demarcation that separates the real from the ideal, the malignant from the benign, and chaos from order, Americans occupy a place that is as precarious as it is privileged. Like it or not, Warren would argue, Americans are charged with forging the link between what is past and what is possible. If we cannot depend upon our literature for answers, we can nevertheless turn to it as we reformulate, on new terms, the covenant of the Founders.

Postscript

On October 9-11, 1985, Louisiana State University was the scene of a major literary event, a conference celebrating the founding of the *Southern Review* on its campus a half-century before.[1] The coeditors of the original series of the *Review*, Brooks and Warren, were there, as were Eudora Welty, Ernest Gaines, and Walker Percy, along with an impressive complement of distinguished authorities on modern letters. It was the presence of Warren, however, that clearly dominated the proceedings. Already visibly ravaged by the illness that would take his life a scant four years later, Warren purportedly came to Baton Rouge against his doctor's orders, and on the evening of his scheduled reading, an overflow crowd packed the large auditorium in the Student Union. Unable to finish his reading, Warren had made prior arrangements for James Olney to complete the program. At its conclusion, the ovation that greeted the poet was unforgettable testimony to the degree to which his work had touched the lives of those present.

The moment was particularly poignant to the author of this book. Several weeks earlier, I had received a long, witty, and informative letter from Warren in response to one of my own routine letters of inquiry. It was only too clear what the writing of that letter had cost Robert Penn Warren, and with some difficulty I managed to get close enough to thank him for it in person. His response, apart from its typical graciousness, was revealing: "I want to thank you. You gave me an opportunity to tell the truth, a rare thing."

For Warren the truth was never simple; nor was it an easy thing to face, much less tell. Yet Warren took the telling of humbling, often agonizing, "truths" as his life's work, convinced that the writer, in charting the dark stream of history, could have a hand in the making of history. Like Jeremiah Beaumont's journal, Warren's canon is addressed to us. In this connection, a passage at the end of *Chief Joseph* might well provide an appropriate note on which to conclude this study. Meditating upon the process of history, which is "Often / Pitiful," but also at times "Triumphant," Warren wonders

> . . . if when the traffic light
> Rings green, some stranger may pause and thus miss
> His own mob's rush to go where the light
> Says go, and pausing, may look,
> Not into a deepening shade of canyon,
> Nor, head up now, toward ice peak in moonlight white,
> But, standing paralyzed in his momentary eternity, into
> His own heart look while he asks
> From what indefinable distance, years, and direction,
> Eyes of fathers are suddenly fixed on him. To know.[2]

This anonymous inmate of the modern city made his first appearance in Warren's work in the Fugitive poem "To a Face in the Crowd." He and his creator had come a long way. Assuming that Wordsworth's sense of the poet as a man speaking to men has, in this era of poststructural theory, a residual validity, it is possible to regard Warren's voluminous and varied literary achievement, informed as it is by his defiantly *American* vision, as the record of a stranger speaking to strangers in a strange land. The message is ultimately one of hope.

Notes

1. Bicentennial in Babylon

1. My discussion is based on the text of "Bicentennial" as it first appeared in *Esquire* (Dec. 1976), 132-35, 200-201.

2. Such characters, reminders of man's bestial side, emerge frequently in Warren's writing. Witness the denizens of Big Hump's island in the 1950 novel *World Enough and Time* and the would-be murderess in *Audubon: A Vision* (1969).

3. *The Poetic Vision of Robert Penn Warren* (Lexington: Univ. Press of Kentucky, 1977), 118.

4. "Mark Twain and the South: An Affair of Love and Anger," *Southern Review* ns 4 (1968): 493-519.

5. "A Conversation with Robert Penn Warren," in Watkins and Hiers, *Robert Penn Warren Talking*, 196, 217. All subsequent references to this and other interviews in the Watkins and Hiers collection are cited parenthetically in the text as *Talking*.

6. Originally an address delivered at Columbia University, "Knowledge and the Image of Man" was published in the *Sewanee Review* 62 (1955): 182-92. It was conveniently reprinted in John L. Longley, Jr., ed., *Robert Penn Warren: A Collection of Critical Essays* (New York: New York Univ. Press, 1965), 237-46. Warren writes, "Man eats of the fruit of the tree of knowledge and falls. But if he takes another bite, he may get at least a sort of redemption" (ibid., 242).

7. *New Republic* (August 23, 1943): 258. Reprinted in William Bedford Clark, ed., *Critical Essays on Robert Penn Warren* (Boston: Hall, 1981), 27-29.

8. Cited in L. Hugh Moore, Jr., *Robert Penn Warren and History: "The Big Myth We Live"* (The Hague: Mouton, 1970), 44.

9. Barnett Guttenberg, *Web of Being: The Novels of Robert Penn Warren* (Nashville: Vanderbilt Univ. Press, 1975), ix-x. Guttenberg has some salient things to say about the parallels between Warren's vision and the thought of Martin Heidegger as well (ix-xiii).

10. One of the best discussions of the impact the Declaration has come to have on the American mind is that of Garry Wills in the Prologue to his *Inventing America: Jefferson's Declaration of Independence* (Garden City, N.Y.: Doubleday, 1978), xiii-xxvi. In my estimation, no one has proven a more astute analyst of the mind of Jefferson and Jefferson's role in the history of mind than Lewis P. Simpson. I would refer the reader to Simpson's *The Dispossessed Garden: Pastoral and History in Southern Literature* (Athens: Univ. of Georgia Press, 1975); "The Ferocity of Self: History and Consciousness in Southern Literature," *South Central Review* 1, nos. 1 and 2 (1984): 67-84; and *Mind and the American Civil War: A Meditation on Lost Causes* (Baton Rouge: Louisiana State Univ. Press, 1989).

11. *The Achievement of Robert Penn Warren* (Baton Rouge: Louisiana State Univ. Press, 1981), 302.

12. I have dealt with this irony in the light of Warren's writings in "Uncle Tom Jefferson's Cabins: Thoughts on Jefferson, Slavery, and the Bicentennial," *Faculty Review of North Carolina A&T State University* (Spring 1976): 78-83. For a much more thorough treatment of Jefferson's views, see John Chester Miller, *The Wolf by the Ears: Thomas Jefferson and Slavery* (New York: Free Press, 1977).

13. In that work Jefferson tells R.P.W. that from the beginning he was aware that "the stench of human action is not always sweetened / By the civet of motive, nor motive by good action," and he assures R.P.W. that "if I held Man innocent, I yet knew / Not all men innocent." See *Brother to Dragons*, 36-37.

14. In an interview with Marshall Walker in 1969, Warren reaffirmed Jefferson's contention that human progress was of necessity gradual: "liberty is gained by inches, so you have to nag along inch by inch." See Walker's *Robert Penn Warren: A Vision Earned* (New York: Barnes & Noble, 1979), 258.

15. Warren's address was part of the fourth series of Franklin Lectures published as *A Time to Hear and Answer: Essays for the Bicentennial Season.* "The Use of the Past" is found on pages 3-35; subsequent references appear parenthetically in the text. The volume features a Preface by Taylor Littleton, and other contributors include O.B. Hardison, Jr., John Archibald Wheeler, Marshall Laird, James Reston, S.I. Hayakawa, and Lynton K. Caldwell.

16. See *The Imperial Self: An Essay in American Literary and Cultural History* (New York: Vintage, 1972). Though Anderson makes no mention of Warren by name, his analysis of what he portrays as the fundamentally pernicious influence of Transcendentalist notions on American culture proceeds from assumptions he instinctively shares with Warren and others among the original group of Nashville Agrarians.

17. Quoted in Strandberg, *Poetic Vision of Robert Penn Warren*, 36.

18. Moore, *Robert Penn Warren and History*, 142.

19. *Yale Review* 27 (1938): 538.

20. Ibid., 542.

21. Warren makes the point that the artist must participate in the

world throughout his work, but nowhere more emphatically than in *Audubon: A Vision* (New York: Random, 1969), 19, where his artist figure is enjoined not only to "walk in the world" but to "love it."

22. MacLeish's words drip with anger:

They screwed her scrawny and gaunt with their seven-year
   panics;
They bought her back on their mortgages old-whore cheap:
They fattened their bonds at her breasts till the thin
   blood ran from them.

See *The Collected Poems of Archibald MacLeish* (Boston: Houghton Mifflin, 1962), 85-86. Toward the very end of his career, Warren would express comparable outrage toward the robber barons of the Gilded Age, who, in his words, "slick-fucked a land" (*Chief Joseph of the Nez Perce* [New York: Random, 1983], 54). For an insightful (if at times thesis-ridden) treatment of the metaphor of the American earth as woman see Annette Kolodny, *The Lay of the Land: Metaphor as Experience and History in American Life and Letters* (Chapel Hill: Univ. of North Carolina Press, 1975).

23. MacLeish shares Warren's assumption that the Declaration of Independence is the principal articulation of the American idea in "National Purpose," *A Continuing Journey* (Boston: Houghton Mifflin, 1967), 77-86.

24. On one level, Niebuhr seems to fault doctrinaire Jeffersonians for the same ahistorical blindness he sees underlying Marxism. See *The Irony of American History* (New York: Scribner's, 1952), 30.

25. MacLeish, *Continuing Journey*, v.

26. In *Continuing Journey*, 141-47. Ironically, MacLeish does not seem to recognize the significance of his coupling the name of Melville's Captain Ahab with those of Franklin, Jefferson, Lincoln, and Emerson.

27. In *The Myth of Southern History: Historical Consciousness in Twentieth-Century Southern Literature* (Nashville: Vanderbilt Univ. Press, 1970), 131-70, F. Garvin Davenport discusses the Niebuhrian quality in Warren's thought and in that of Warren's friend, the southern historian C. Vann Woodward.

28. At first, the linking of Warren to James may seem off the mark, especially in light of the former's guarded appraisal of the protopragmatism of the North during and after the Civil War: "This was the state of mind that saw history not in terms of abstract, fixed principles but as a wavering flow of shifting values and contingencies, each to be confronted on the terms of its context" (*Jefferson Davis Gets His Citizenship Back* [Lexington: Univ. Press of Kentucky, 1980], 62). Yet Warren, like his fellow Agrarians, always eschewed abstractions in favor of concrete particulars, and an untempered abstract idealism leads to the undoing of many of his protagonists. Cushing Strout has skillfully demonstrated the presence of William James in Warren's greatest novel in *"All the King's Men* and the Shadow of William James," *Southern Review* ns 6 (1970): 920-34 (reprinted in Clark, *Critical Essays on Robert Penn Warren*, 160-71). Another Warren critic, Strandberg, even goes so far as to acknowledge James as the

"guiding spirit" behind his *Poetic Vision of Robert Penn Warren* (ix). Per-haps the best overview of James's thought is that of John J. McDermott in the Introduction to his *The Writings of William James: A Comprehensive Edition* (Chicago: Univ. of Chicago Press, 1977), xix-liv. Though McDer-mott does not mention Warren, certain of his observations about James hold a particular interest for students of Warren (see, for instance, xi, xii, xv, xxi, xliii, xlvii, xlviii).

2. A 1920s Apprenticeship

1. *Only Yesterday: An Informal History of the Nineteen-Twenties* (1931; New York: Perennial Library, 1964), vii. Allen was fully aware that "con-temporary history is bound to be anything but definitive." Nevertheless, his book remains something of a minor classic of American letters.

2. See for example John M. Bradbury, *The Fugitives: A Critical Ac-count* (Chapel Hill: Univ. of North Carolina Press, 1958); Louise Cowan, *The Fugitive Group: A Literary History* (Baton Rouge: Louisiana State Univ. Press, 1959); John L. Stewart, *The Burden of Time: The Fugitives and Agrarians* (Princeton: Princeton Univ. Press, 1965); and Alexander Ka-ranikas, *Tillers of a Myth: Southern Agrarians as Social and Literary Critics* (Madison: Univ. of Wisconsin Press, 1966).

3. Frederick J. Hoffman, *The Twenties: American Writing in the Post-war Decade* (New York: Viking, 1955), 426; Richard M. Ludwig and Clifford A. Nault, Jr., eds., *Annals of American Literature* (New York: Oxford Univ. Press, 1986).

4. *Driftwood Flames* (Nashville: Nashville Poetry Guild, 1923), 10.

5. Ibid., 36-37.

6. *Fugitive* 2 (June-July 1923): 90-91.

7. Charles H. Bohner, *Robert Penn Warren* (New York: Twayne, 1964), 42.

8. *Fugitive* 3 (Apr. 1924): 54.

9. *Fugitive* 4 (June 1925): 36. This poem remained significant to War-ren throughout his career, turning up in all the subsequent volumes of his collected verse. In keeping with Warren's practice of presenting his poems in reverse chronology, it appears as the final work in *New and Selected Poems, 1923-1985* (New York: Random, 1985).

10. *The Wary Fugitives: Four Poets and the South* (Baton Rouge: Loui-siana State Univ. Press, 1978), 331.

11. Written at Oxford where Warren was in residence as a Rhodes Scholar, "Prime Leaf" opened up new creative dimensions for the young poet and confirmed his talent for fiction. See Warren's *Paris Review* inter-view, included in Watkins and Hiers, *Robert Penn Warren Talking*, 35.

12. See also the companion piece, "August Revival: Crosby Junction" (*Sewanee Review* 33 [1925]: 439). Taken together, these two poems demon-strate the youthful Warren's struggle with the dialectic of belief and doubt that became an important factor in his later writing.

13. Stewart, *Burden of Time*, 438-39.

14. James B. Meriwether and Michael Millgate, eds., *Lion in the Garden: Interviews with William Faulkner* (New York: Random, 1968), 255.

15. Warren objected *profanely* to the title. See Thomas Daniel Young, *Waking Their Neighbors Up: The Nashville Agrarians Reconsidered* (Athens: Univ. of Georgia Press, 1982), 17-18.

16. *I'll Take My Stand*, xlv. Subsequent references appear in the text.

17. *All the King's Men*, 436.

18. I concur fully with William C. Havard's "The Politics of *I'll Take My Stand*," *Southern Review* 16 (1980): 757-75. Havard has coedited, with Walter Sullivan, an important retrospective on the Agrarian symposium, *A Band of Prophets: The Vanderbilt Agrarians After Fifty Years* (Baton Rouge: Louisiana State Univ. Press, 1982). See especially the essays by Lewis P. Simpson, Robert B. Heilman, and Louis D. Rubin, Jr.

19. Rob Roy Purdy, ed., *The Fugitives' Reunion: Conversations at Vanderbilt, May 3-5, 1956* (Nashville: Vanderbilt Univ. Press, 1959), 213.

20. As Rubin points out, "The Briar Patch" has "satisfied nobody, least of all Warren" (*Wary Fugitives*, 216). Little good is served by the (quite uncharacteristic) harshness of James H. Justus's criticism of the essay in *Achievement of Robert Penn Warren*, 138-42. My approach is more in keeping with that of Marshall Walker, who sees in "The Briar Patch" an informing "moral realism" (*Robert Penn Warren: A Vision Earned*, 34-35).

21. Havard, in "The Politics of *I'll Take My Stand*," 769, rightfully notes that Warren's stress on the need for black Americans to "establish their identity as members of a black community on the way to establishing identity as human beings" parallels the later stance of men like Martin Luther King, Jr., and Jesse Jackson.

22. In a 1974 interview with Marshall Walker, Warren went so far as to voice his "sympathies" with that sometimes unruly offspring of Black Pride—*Black Power*—recognizing that it emerged from a valid "psychological need." Warren added, "I think I know quite enough about Southern chauvinism to understand black chauvinism." In Watkins and Hiers, *Robert Penn Warren Talking*, 191.

23. On July 21, 1930, Davidson wrote Tate: "I was rather shocked by Red's essay. It hardly seems worthy of Red, or worthy of the subject. . . . Furthermore, the ideas advanced about the negro don't seem to chime with our ideas as I understand them. Behind the essay, too, are implications which I am sure we won't accept—they are 'progressive' implications, with a pretty strong smack of latter-day sociology. . . . I simply can't understand what Red is after here. It doesn't sound like Red at all—at least not the Red Warren I know. The very language, the catchwords, somehow don't fit. I am almost inclined to doubt whether RED ACTUALLY WROTE THIS ESSAY!" Davidson urged Tate to consider excluding "The Briar Patch" from *I'll Take My Stand*. John Tyree Fain and Thomas Daniel Young, eds., *The Literary Correspondence of Donald Davidson and Allen Tate* (Athens: Univ. of Georgia Press, 1974), 125.

24. See my "'Secret Sharers' in Warren's Later Fiction," in James A. Grimshaw, Jr., ed., *"Time's Glory": Original Essays on Robert Penn Warren* (Conway. Univ. of Central Arkansas Press, 1986), 65-76.

25. Consult the annotated entries in Neil Nakadate's *Robert Penn Warren: A Reference Guide* (Boston: Hall, 1977). For a narrative account of Warren's evolving critical reputation see the Introduction to my *Critical Essays on Robert Penn Warren*, 1-18.

26. Allan Nevins, "Martyr and Fanatic," *New Republic*, 19 Mar. 1930: 134-35; reprinted in Clark, *Critical Essays on Robert Penn Warren*, 21-23. Nevins praised *John Brown* to Warren as late as the 1950s and urged him to bring the book back into print (Letter from RPW to William Bedford Clark, Feb. 7, 1981).

27. An Emersonian, Bloom takes umbrage at Warren's working assumptions in *John Brown*. See his Introduction to the Modern Critical Views volume *Robert Penn Warren* (New York: Chelsea, 1986), 2.

28. Thomas L. Connelley, "Robert Penn Warren as Historian," in Walter B. Edgar, ed., *A Southern Renascence Man: Views of Robert Penn Warren* (Baton Rouge: Louisiana State Univ. Press, 1984), 7.

29. It is difficult not to agree with Rubin that "Tate had already decided what Jackson's and Davis's lives were supposed to mean before he began the books, and mainly he worked at fitting the biographical material into his thesis" (*Wary Fugitives*, 98).

30. *Stonewall Jackson*, 33. Subsequent references appear in the text.

31. It seems likely that the complexities presented by Lee's personality and career were responsible for Tate's decision not to pursue his intended biography of the man, but Robert S. Dupree's speculations on this point are worth considering (*Allen Tate and the Augustinian Imagination: A Study of the Poetry* [Baton Rouge: Louisiana State Univ. Press, 1983], 116-17).

32. Radcliffe Squires is right when he suggests that the tragic paradigm that informs Tate's portrait of Davis is meant to mirror the divisions of a doomed culture. See *Allen Tate: A Literary Biography* (New York: Pegasus, 1971), 99.

33. *Jefferson Davis: His Rise and Fall* (New York: Minton, Balch, 1929), 8.

34. Tate, *Jefferson Davis*, 256, 259.

35. Marshall Walker puts it well in *Robert Penn Warren: A Vision Earned*, 237: "With *John Brown: The Making of a Martyr*, Warren demonstrated the readiness to 'enter history, not flinch from history' that has typified his career."

36. It is important to recall that Stephen Vincent Benét published *John Brown's Body* in 1927, just as Warren was beginning his biography. Benét's sprawling verse epic was one of the most celebrated poems of the 1920s, though the vogue of Pound and Eliot modernism gradually consigned it to relative oblivion. Benét, like Warren, refused to sentimentalize Brown or downplay the complex ironies of his personality and actions, and his portrait of Brown, drawn from many of the same sources, anticipates Warren's. (Warren denied any direct influence, though he did admit that he envied Benét his title [Letter to William Bedford Clark, Oct. 9, 1986].) In any event, Benét, for all his desire to penetrate the public mask of Brown, finally translates him into symbol: the embodiment of an

historical force that cannot be resisted. Warren, characteristically, refuses to confuse John Brown with the zeitgeist. He insists, first and last, that Brown was a man, in no way reducible to an imaginative construct (for all his self-dramatization).

37. Bohner, *Robert Penn Warren*, 29; Rubin, *Wary Fugitives*, 336.

38. Justus is one of many commentators who see Brown as a prototype of later protagonists in Warren's fiction (*Achievement of Robert Penn Warren*, 209-10.) Warren indicated to Walker that Brown "had some kind of constant obsessive interest for me," and the nagging paradox of Brown clearly remained a problem with which Warren wrestled long after the publication of his first book:

On the one hand, he's so heroic; on the other hand he's so vile. . . . Some fifteen years ago, when Edmund Wilson was working on *Patriotic Gore*, we'd meet at parties and he would say, "Red, let's go . . . and talk about the Civil War," and we always did. And the subject of Brown once or twice came up, and he once said, "But he's trivial, he's merely a homicidal maniac—forget him!" Now this is *half* of Brown. In a strange way the homicidal maniac lives in terms of grand gestures and heroic stances . . . but *is* a homicidal maniac! This is a strange situation; and the split of feeling around Brown makes the split of feeling in a thing like my character Stark [in *All the King's Men*] almost trivial. Brown lives in the dramatic stance of his life, rather than in the psychological content of it; he lives in noble stances and noble utterances, and at the psychological and often the *factual* level of conduct was . . . brutal. Perfect self-deception—yet "noble." Now on this point, I suppose, the people I have chosen to write about—or rather, who have chosen me to write about *them*—are trying to find out some way to make these things work together, come together: somehow they are trying to get out of this box. This would be true of a man like the hero of *World Enough and Time*, who *must* find a *cause*, an ideal cause, in order to justify some of his most secret and destructive motives—no, that's not accurate—*needs*. (Watkins and Hiers, *Robert Penn Warren Talking*, 181-82)

39. *John Brown*, 446. Subsequent references appear in the text.

40. We can only speculate as to the measure of identification Warren may have felt with his subject in this regard, given the fact that a devastating eye injury prevented him from pursuing a projected naval career. See Floyd C. Watkins, *Then and Now: The Personal Past in the Poetry of Robert Penn Warren* (Lexington: Univ. Press of Kentucky, 1982), 54-56. The motif of blindness, total or partial, haunts Warren's writing, and it is perhaps significant that the nameless Indian in *Audubon*, the artist/hero's dark double, has lost an eye in a senseless accident.

41. *All the King's Men* (1946; New York: Harcourt Brace Jovanovich, 1974), 436.

42. See James A. Grimshaw, Jr.'s indispensable *Robert Penn Warren: A Descriptive Bibliography* (Charlottesville: Univ. Press of Virginia, 1981), 265.

43. Watkins and Hiers, *Robert Penn Warren Talking*, 185.

3. Out of the Thirties

1. "Passage to India" dates from 1871, the same year as *Democratic Vistas*, in which Whitman expresses some gloomy reservations as to the future of America in the new age. In the light of such reservations, "Passage to India" seems at times like a kind of whistling in the dark.

2. "Empire," *This Quarter* 3, n. 1 (1930): 169.

3. Edwin Thomas Wood, "On Native Soil: A Talk with Robert Penn Warren," *Mississippi Quarterly* 37 (Spring 1984): 183.

4. *You Can't Go Home Again* (1940; reprint, Garden City, N.Y.: Sun Dial, 1942), 414.

5. For a recent discussion of Wolfe's relatively naive politics during the Depression, see David Herbert Donald, *Look Homeward: A Life of Thomas Wolfe* (Boston: Little, Brown, 1987), 303-05, 354-62, 434-38.

6. Stephen W. Baskerville and Ralph Willett, eds., *Nothing to Fear: New Perspectives on America in the Thirties* (Manchester, England: Manchester Univ. Press, 1985), 5.

7. *The Great Depression: America, 1929-1941* (New York: Times Books, 1984), 205.

8. Following Alexander Karanikas's assessment of the Agrarians for the most part, Webster uses the term Tory Formalist to describe, somewhat reductively, "a group of men who believe in or wish for a social and intellectual world and a literature that express belief in tradition, order, hierarchy, the fallen nature of man, the war of good and evil, and the ultimate union of warring dualisms in the Word of God and the metaphors of poetry." See *The Republic of Letters: A History of Postwar American Criticism* (Baltimore: Johns Hopkins Univ. Press, 1979), 63.

9. Thomas W. Cutrer's *Parnassus on the Mississippi: The Southern Review and the Baton Rouge Literary Community, 1935-1942* (Baton Rouge: Louisiana State Univ. Press, 1984) is an indispensable source of information on Warren's career in the 1930s.

10. *Proletarian Literature in the United States: An Anthology* (New York: International, 1935), 29.

11. While admitting in his essay "Archibald MacLeish" that there were "obvious objections" to identifying MacLeish's liberal poetry as fascist, Obed Brooks nevertheless registered an uneasiness about the implications of MacLeish's verse: "One can imagine how the terror, the authority, the ritual, the patriotism—subrational and impulsive—that he has so constantly sought outside himself, could come at last with the marching feet of the storm troops" (*Proletarian Literature*, 329).

12. *Proletarian Literature*, 171.

13. The *New Republic* (July 15, 1936): 304.

14. As John Burt notes, the appeal to a "higher law," for Warren, is uncomfortably close to "the appeal to force." A "high moral intent" too often affects "the repeal of morality." See *Robert Penn Warren and American Idealism* (New Haven, Conn.: Yale Univ. Press, 1988), 29.

15. The earliest of the poems in the collection, "To a Face in the

Crowd," no doubt assumed an enhanced power by virtue of its reappearance in the midst of the Depression. Its mood of urban alienation must have struck more than one responsive chord. Allen Tate confessed a special feeling for this Fugitive poem, despite reservations, and reluctantly approved its inclusion in *Thirty-Six Poems* (Letter to RPW, Jan. 27, 1935; Robert Penn Warren Papers, Beinecke Rare Book and Manuscript Library, Yale University).

16. For a brief account of the poem's genesis, see Burt, *Robert Penn Warren and American Idealism*, 76.

17. *Thirty-Six Poems*, 10. Subsequent citations to this edition appear in the text.

18. *Robert Penn Warren and American Idealism*, 112.

19. *Poems* (New York: Scribner's, 1960), 23.

20. Schlesinger's *The Cycles of American History* (Boston: Houghton Mifflin, 1986) is informed by attitudes that Warren would have embraced in the main, though he might have balked at certain of Schlesinger's applications of principle. Schlesinger, like Warren, is outspokenly suspicious of ideology, but he remains something of a New Deal/New Frontier ideologue nonetheless.

21. Motives are usually complex, and Cowley has suggested that many writers welcomed a commitment to radical politics as a way "to escape from a feeling of isolation and ineffectuality. They wanted to merge themselves in some great aggregation of suffering men and women" (—*And I Worked at the Writer's Trade: Chapters of Literary History, 1918-1978* [New York: Viking, 1978], 100). Politics led to some violent partisanships pitting writers against one another in the 1930s, but oftentimes a common devotion to literature and a sharing in the difficulties attendant upon the writer's calling superseded political differences. Both Cowley and Wilson, though they generally regarded Agrarianism with bemused condescension, were on particularly good terms with Allen Tate, even visiting him and his wife, Caroline Gordon, in Tennessee. Cowley worked on *Exile's Return* while staying with Gordon's Meriwether kin. See Cowley's *The Dream of the Golden Mountains: Remembering the 1930s* (New York: Viking, 1980), Chapter 17. *The Dream of the Golden Mountains* is itself dedicated to Robert Penn Warren. For all their differences, both Marxists and Agrarians, as Joel Wingard has written, saw industrial capitalism as dehumanizing and "sought to respond to the modern social disharmony by advocating a unified culture to be achieved through social cooperation and the integration of artist and society." See "'Folded in a Single Party':Agrarians and Proletarians," *Southern Review* ns 16 (1980): 776-81.

22. *Cycles of American History*, 19.

23. Herbert Agar, who coedited *Who Owns America?* with Tate, might have been speaking for Warren when he described the self-fulfilling perils of deterministic thought: "There is a large element of truth in deterministic theories of history. If a society is morally inert . . . it will tend to function mechanically, and its future will be as predictable as the workings of any other machine. The difference between a moral agent and

a machine is that the moral agent has choice. Man has the power to make himself a moral agent, but he need not use that power. If his self-awareness (his consciousness of his own desires and motives) be torpid, he will become the next thing to a machine . . . and a society composed chiefly of such units will have the minimum of moral will." See Agar's "The Task for Conservatism," *American Review* 3 (1934): 3.

24. *Robert Penn Warren and American Idealism*, 65-66.

25. "Literature as a Symptom," in Agar and Tate, *Who Owns America?*, 267. Subsequent references appear parenthetically in the text.

26. Ransom's assertion that the nature of a poem is akin to that of "a democratic state" while "prose discourse" approximates "a totalitarian state" makes this correspondence between poetics and politics quite clear. See "Criticism as Pure Speculation," in Thomas Daniel Young and John Hindle, eds., *Selected Essays of John Crowe Ransom* (Baton Rouge: Louisiana State Univ. Press, 1984), 137.

27. "Edna Millay's Maturity," *Southwest Review* 20 (July 1935): Book Supplement, 3. The Book Supplement of this issue was edited by Brooks and Warren as part of a brief arrangement between Pipkin at LSU and the *Southwest Review* editors at Southern Methodist University. See Cutrer, *Parnassus on the Mississippi*, 31-49.

28. Cleanth Brooks interviewed by William Bedford Clark in New Haven, Aug. 23, 1988. See also Cutrer, *Parnassus on the Mississippi*, 77-105, *passim*.

29. *Southern Review* 1 (1935-36): 1.

30. Brooks felt he and Warren served the interests of young and unknown southerners best by publishing their work in the company of writers of national and international stature rather than by extolling regional pieties—"playing Dixie," in Brooks's phrase. Cleanth Brooks interviewed by William Bedford Clark in New Haven, Aug. 23, 1988.

31. *Southern Review* 1 (1935-36): 320.

32. "Art and the Revolutionary Attitude," *Southern Review* 1 (1935-36): 239-40.

33. Tate's defensiveness in the face of opposing political thought seemed to stiffen as the 1930s progressed, but in 1931 he had written Warren and Davidson in an attempt to enlist their support for a group of radical writers charged with criminal syndicalism in Kentucky. He suggested that all writers had an interest in protecting free speech, even as he insisted on the importance of dissociating oneself from the offensive politics of the writers in question (Letter of Dec. 10, 1931; Warren Papers). See also Paul K. Conkin, *The Southern Agrarians* (Knoxville: Univ. of Tennessee Press, 1988), 94.

34. *Southern Review* 1 (1935-36): 559.

35. Warren Papers.

36. "Dixie Looks at Mrs. Gerould," *American Review* 6 (1936): 387.

37. See Albert E. Stone, Jr., "Seward Collins and the *American Review*: Experiment in Pro-Fascism," *American Quarterly* 12 (1960): 4-19.

38. See Conkin, *Southern Agrarians*, 106-10. Conkin misidentifies Grace Lumpkin as Kate Lumpkin.

39. In *The Rise of the New York Intellectuals: Partisan Review and Its Circle, 1934-1945* (Madison: Univ. of Wisconsin Press, 1986), Terry A. Cooney has provided a detailed history of the magazine and the writers most closely associated with it. It is useful to see Rahv and Phillips as leftist counterparts of Brooks and Warren. A shared desire to promote modern letters fostered a mutual respect between the two sets of editors according to Brooks. Interviewed by William Bedford Clark in New Haven, Aug. 23, 1988.

40. See Cutrer, *Parnassus on the Mississippi*, 213-55. The war was only an ostensible excuse for suspending institutional support of the quarterly. The demise of the *Southern Review* provides an object lesson in misplaced academic priorities and administrative bungling on the part of university officials.

41. *Southern Review* 7 (Spring 1942): n.p.

42. See, for example, Cowley's confession of complicity in supporting the Stalinist purges: "Echoes from Moscow: 1937-1938," *Southern Review* ns 20 (1984): 1-11.

43. "Arnold vs. the 19th Century," *Kenyon Review* 1 (1939): 219.

44. *Eleven Poems on the Same Theme*, [2]. The edition is not paginated. Subsequent references will appear in the text.

45. "Proud Flesh" is the title of several unpublished versions of a play that eventually became *All the King's Men*. Warren meant the title to be doubly significant ("A Note on *All the King's Men*," *Sewanee Review* 61 [1953], 477). The title of *All the King's Men* may, in turn, have been obliquely suggested by an essay of R.K. Gooch ("Humpty Dumpty and the Dictators," *Southern Review* 2 [1936-37]: 774-82).

46. It is true that Warren was quoted in 1939 to the effect that "if we get into the next war we are suckers" (*Partisan Review* 6 [1939]: 113). However, this response was to a question posed long before Hitler's invasion of Poland in September of that year. "Terror" was copyrighted in February 1941 and clearly reflects a rejection of isolationist sentiments. (Pearl Harbor was not quite a year away.) For the circumstances surrounding the poem's composition see Charles Bohner, *Robert Penn Warren*, revised edition (Boston: Twayne, 1981), 41-42.

47. Calvin Bedient goes so far as to assert that Warren's "greatness as a writer" dates from *Audubon* (1969); see *In the Heart's Last Kingdom: Robert Penn Warren's Major Poetry* (Cambridge: Harvard Univ. Press, 1984), 3. Like most of Bedient's judgments, such a pronouncement says much more about him than about Warren.

48. Frank Jones, "A Poet," *Nation* (Sept. 26, 1942): 277. See also Louis Untermeyer ("Cream of the Verse," *Yale Review* 32 [1942-43]: 366-71), who says of these poems, "it is the history of mind which is being searched."

49. Alfred Kazin on fellow leftist Mary McCarthy: "her moving principle was that bleak, unsparing, suspicious view of human nature which is so much admired by reactionaries because it leaves the lower classes so little reason to rebel" (*Starting Out in the Thirties* [New York: Vintage, 1980], 156). Kazin's grasp of the theological and psychological implications of the doctrine of Original Sin is inadequate. Indeed, much of Amer-

ica's reforming impulse can be traced to the Puritans, who were steeped in Augustinianism. See Paul K. Conkin, *Puritans and Pragmatists: Eight Eminent American Thinkers* (Bloomington: Indiana Univ. Press, 1976), 12-14.

50. James Agee and Walker Evans, *Let Us Now Praise Famous Men* (1941; Boston: Houghton Mifflin, 1980), 249-50.

51. Agee aimed at "truth" that would transcend simple "journalism." See David P. Peeler's valuable *Hope Among Us Yet: Social Criticism and Social Solace in Depression America* (Athens: Univ. of Georgia Press, 1987), 50-55.

52. In response to a *Partisan Review* questionnaire mailed to various writers (note 46, above), Warren indicated that he had "been in sympathy" with the protests behind much 1930s literature, though the literature itself left a good deal to be desired. (This same questionnaire infuriated Agee. See Agee and Evans, *Let Us Now Praise Famous Men*, 349-57.) By the same token, in his 1974 Jefferson Lecture, published as *Democracy and Poetry*, Warren asserted that no one "who . . . lived through the Great Depression" could agree with Henry James that art in itself constituted a "justification of all life" or fail to recognize the social suffering of "many millions of human beings" (91).

53. "Christmas Gift," in *The Circus in the Attic and Other Stories* (New York: Harcourt Brace, 1947), 104.

54. As readers of Faulkner's *The Sound and the Fury* and *Sartoris* will remember, the southern vernacular phrase "Christmas Gift" is sometimes used to solicit a present or contribution. The significance of Warren's title becomes clear in this final scene, in which communion replaces charity.

55. One of the most familiar—and powerful of these photographic images, Rothstein's "Farmer and Sons Walking in the Face of a Dust Storm," was not staged, but Rothstein admitted that he would have staged it if reality itself had not provided the adequate elements necessary to his statement (Peeler, *Hope Among Us Yet*, 95). Diana Trilling evoked the name of Walker Evans in reviewing *All the King's Men* ("Fiction in Review," *Nation* [Aug. 24, 1946]: 220). See L. Hugh Moore, Jr., *Robert Penn Warren and History: "The Big Myth We Live"* (The Hague: Mouton, 1970), 45.

56. Warren's "T.S. Stribling: A Paragraph in the History of Critical Realism," *American Review* 2 (1934): 463-86, is a classic formulation of Warren's position with respect to reductivist art. It bears comparison with his influential essay "Pure and Impure Poetry," *Kenyon Review* 5 (1943): 228-54.

57. In the face of the conversion of many of his friends to the new Marxist faith, that student of the "modern temper" Joseph Wood Krutch felt like a pagan at the dawn of the Christian age (John D. Margolis, *Joseph Wood Krutch: A Writer's Life* [Knoxville: Univ. of Tennessee Press, 1980], 108).

58. "'All the King's Men': The Matrix of Experience," *Yale Review* ns 53 (1963-64): 162.

4. Democracy and "Soulcraft"

1. *Night Rider*, 2-3. Subsequent references will appear in the text. Richard G. Law and others have rightly noted the degree to which the opening scene of the novel "presages" the entire action ("Warren's *Night Rider* and the Issue of Naturalism: The 'Nightmare' of Our Age," *Southern Literary Journal* 8, n. 2 [1976]: 41-61).

2. As Allen Shepherd observes, "The self cannot be truly fulfilled unless it is drawn out of itself into the life of another." See "Robert Penn Warren as a Philosophical Novelist," reprinted in Harold Bloom, ed., *Robert Penn Warren's* All the King's Men: *Modern Critical Interpretations* (New York: Chelsea, 1987), 60. Warren's relationship with his assumed reader, "you," is obviously governed by the same principle. See Simone Vauthier, "The Case of the Vanishing Narratee: An Inquiry into *All the King's Men*," *Southern Literary Journal* 6, n. 2 (1974): 42-69.

3. My understanding of the significance of "collectivities" is much influenced by Catherine Savage Brosman, "Theories of Collectivities in Sartre and Rousseau," *South Central Review* 2, n. 1 (1985): 25-41.

4. James H. Justus discusses this aspect of the early fiction in *Achievement of Robert Penn Warren*, 159-63.

5. "September 1, 1939," in *The Collected Poetry of W.H. Auden* (New York: Random, 1945), 57. Justus cites a passage from "In Memory of W.B. Yeats" in a somewhat similar context in *Achievement of Robert Penn Warren*, 205.

6. *The Glass Menagerie* (New York: New Directions, 1970), 115. Williams's play was first performed in December 1944.

7. "Tragic Liberal," *New Republic* (May 31, 1939): 108. Reprinted in Clark, *Critical Essays on Robert Penn Warren*, 26-27.

8. "The Regional Novel: The Example of Robert Penn Warren," *Sewanee Review* 53 (1945): 84-102. In his fine early discussion of the novel, Leonard Casper felt it necessary to assert that *Night Rider* was more than "an indictment of proto-fascist terrorism" (*Robert Penn Warren: The Dark and Bloody Ground* [Seattle: Univ. of Washington Press, 1960], 101).

9. John Stone and Stephen Mennell, eds., *Alexis de Tocqueville on Democracy, Revolution, and Society: Selected Writings* (Chicago: Univ. of Chicago Press, 1980), 82.

10. Ibid., 81-82.

11. Ibid., 84.

12. Warren shared with John Winthrop a sense of the distinction between "natural" and "civil" liberty. See Russell B. Nye and Norman S. Grabo, eds., *American Thought and Writing* (Boston: Houghton Mifflin, 1965), 1: 60-61. He would, however, have had obvious trouble with Winthrop's overreliance on a supposedly benign "authority."

13. Alvan S. Ryan's "Robert Penn Warren's *Night Rider*: The Nihilism of the Isolated Temperament," *Modern Fiction Studies* 7 (1961-62): 338-46, remains one of the best readings of the novel as a "philosophical" fiction.

14. Munn takes a perverse pleasure in tormenting May in little ways,

both physically and verbally, long before he works his aggressive will on her to the fullest. The element of sadistic sexuality reasserts itself frequently throughout the Warren canon. We should remember Jeremiah Beaumont's masturbatory fantasies involving the young female martyr in *World Enough and Time* (1950) and Audubon's sexual arousal during the hanging of the woman in *Audubon: A Vision* (1969). A feminist critic of my acquaintance, equating Warren with his characters, finds such passages offensive and disturbing.

15. In a slightly different context, Chester E. Eisinger makes this point in *Fiction of the Forties* (Chicago: Univ. of Chicago Press, 1963), 4. See also Warren French, *The Social Novel at the End of an Era* (Carbondale: Southern Illinois Univ. Press, 1966), 188. Writing in the *American Mercury* for December 1939, James T. Farrell surveyed the politics of the novel during the 1930s and observed, "One of the finest American first novels of many years is Robert Penn Warren's *Night Rider*, which portrays a social struggle with insight and without sacrificing individual characterization to didacticism." See "The End of a Literary Decade," reprinted in Ralph F. Bogardus and Fred Hobson, eds., *Literature at the Barricades: The American Writer in the 1930s* (University: Univ. of Alabama Press, 1982), 205.

16. In an omnibus review of new novels, Philip Rahv, whose leftist credentials were hardly in question, called *Night Rider* "patently the most distinguished work on my list," even as he found *The Grapes of Wrath* terribly flawed (*Partisan Review* 6, n. 3 [1939], 112). Kenneth Burke, always on top of things, linked the two novels together in *The Philosophy of Literary Form: Studies in Symbolic Action* (Baton Rouge: Louisiana State Univ. Press, 1941), 81.

17. Warren's paradigm for the failed revolution was, of course, the Confederate Lost Cause, and he had an embodiment of the moral ambiguity of such an enterprise in the person of his maternal grandfather, Gabriel Telemachus Penn, an obvious model for Captain Todd in *Night Rider*. See the poem "Court-martial" in *Promises: Poems 1954-1956* (New York: Random, 1957).

18. The classic treatment of Warren's brand of cosmic consciousness is that of Victor Strandberg in "Warren's Osmosis," *Criticism* 10 (1968): 23-40. Reprinted in Clark, *Critical Essays on Robert Penn Warren*, 122-36.

19. *Regeneration Through Violence: The Mythology of the American Frontier, 1660-1860* (Middletown, Conn.: Wesleyan Univ. Press, 1973).

20. Barnett Guttenberg is among the critics who raise such a possibility in his *Web of Being*, 14. On the question of whether or not Munn's death is a deliberate "suicide," as some readers maintain, see Burke, *Philosophy of Literary Form*, 81.

21. Justus, "On the Politics of the Self-Created: *At Heaven's Gate*," *Sewanee Review* 82 (1974): 284-99 (later incorporated into *Achievement of Robert Penn Warren*); Law, "*At Heaven's Gate*: The Fires of Irony," *American Literature* 53 (1981): 87-104.

22. "Self-Knowledge, the Pearl of Pus, and the Seventh Circle," in

Longley's *Robert Penn Warren: A Collection of Critical Essays* (New York: New York Univ. Press, 1965), 60-74.

23. Ibid., 61.

24. "An Interview with Robert Penn Warren," in Watkins and Hiers, *Robert Penn Warren Talking*, 234. Warren read Dante at LSU along with his student Robert Lowell, who did—for a time—convert. The Catholic chaplain at the university, the Reverend Maurice Schexnayder, who became a bishop, loaned Lowell books on theology, which he discussed with Warren over lunch in the offices of the *Southern Review.* See Cutrer, *Parnassus on the Mississippi*, 198. See also David Farrell, "Reminiscences: A Conversation with Robert Penn Warren," *Southern Review* ns 16 (1980): 797.

25. See Casper, *Robert Penn Warren*, 115; Allen Shepherd, "The Poles of Fiction: Warren's *At Heaven's Gate*," *Texas Studies in Literature and Language* 12 (1971): 709-18.

26. George F. Will, *Statecraft as Soulcraft: What Government Does* (New York: Simon and Schuster, 1983). Will quotes Warren on Abraham Lincoln (54-55).

27. *At Heaven's Gate*, 21-22. Subsequent references appear parenthetically in the text.

28. The bellboy is suspicious of his motives. The full irony of this fact is only manifest after one reads the parallel scene with Sarrett, Jerry's alter ego and indeed a homosexual.

29. One might recall the place amateur athletics plays in Thorstein Veblen's *The Theory of the Leisure Class* (1899). The contemporary reader of *At Heaven's Gate* must be struck by the relevance of the scene in which Murdock discusses the need to professionalize college football (20).

30. Warren's portrait of the emperor should be consulted: "Tiberius on Capri," in *You, Emperors, and Others: Poems 1957-1960* (New York: Random, 1960), 22-23. For discussion of this poem, see Floyd C. Watkins, "Robert Penn Warren's Roman Emperors: You and the Emperors," *Essays in Literature* 10 (1983): 255-61. In comparing the orgy of consumerism in contemporary America to the unbridled gluttony of a Roman emperor (in his verse prologue to *Homage to Theodore Dreiser* [1971]), Warren again demonstrated just how far the nation had abandoned the model of *republican* Rome that had "hung in the air for Jefferson as he penned the Declaration" (*Democracy and Poetry*, xv).

31. Uncle Lew's vitriolic and scornful brand of satire, tied as it is to his own physical handicap, recalls that of Shakespeare's "deformed and scurrilous" Thersites in *Troilus and Cressida*, much as Duckfoot Blake's manic irony resembles that of Mercutio in *Romeo and Juliet*. (Mercutio stands for the subversive poetic impulse in Warren's essay "Pure and Impure Poetry.") Warren's frequent appropriation of Shakespearian elements throughout his canon deserves full treatment in its own right. Mark Royden Winchell makes a tentative beginning in "Renaissance Men: Shakespeare's Influence on Robert Penn Warren," in Philip C. Kolin, ed., *Shakespeare and Southern Writers: A Study in Influence* (Jackson: Univ. Press of Mississippi, 1985), 137-58.

32. Casper, for instance, sees Murdock as "incapable of qualms" (*Robert Penn Warren*, 112). Even Longley oversimplifies Murdock, describing him as a "completely fulfilled nihilist consciously posing as the last Renaissance man" ("Self-Knowledge," 66).

33. "Hemingway," *Kenyon Review* 9 (1947): 1-28, later reprinted in Warren's *Selected Essays* (New York: Random, 1958), 80-118.

34. *Robert Penn Warren: A Vision Earned*, 97.

35. *All The King's Men* (1946; New York: Harcourt Brace Jovanovich, 1982), 7. Subsequent references are to this readily available edition.

36. *Robert Penn Warren and the American Imagination* (Athens: Univ. of Georgia Press, 1990), 19-20. I profited much from the opportunity to read Professor Ruppersburg's study in typescript.

37. Warren embraces democracy almost by default it seems at times, rather like those Founders of the Republic whose mistrust of concentrating power in fallible human hands necessitated its diffusion within a system of checks and balances. For a different sense of this problem in democratic polity (based on the insights of Garry Wills) see Burt, *Robert Penn Warren and American Idealism*, 22-23.

38. The name Lucy is well-chosen. Lucy Lewis, Jefferson's sister, performs a similar function in *Brother to Dragons*, when she insists that Jefferson must come to accept his murderous nephew Lilburne if he is to come to terms with himself. (Happily, history provided Warren with a symbolically-charged name in this latter instance.) It is perhaps worth noting that Audubon's wife was also named Lucy. Following the "logic" of Warren's "name-game," Lucille Christian in *Night Rider* offers little light to Perse Munn.

39. Burt writes in *Robert Penn Warren and American Idealism* (171): "The affirmation of *All the King's Men* is a fresh apprehension of value, not as a guide to action, but as an occasion for integrity in the face of one's inevitable failures to connect value and action. To understand value is not to find one's bearings in the world but rather to understand what it is to discover that one can never do so, to understand how one behaves under those circumstances, and to understand that that behavior is itself a form of value. . . . The book closes with affirmation, but it is perhaps an affirmation only available once there is nothing to affirm."

40. See Justus on the historical significance of the novel's conclusion (*Achievement of Robert Penn Warren*, 204-6).

41. Here I follow the persuasive insights of Strout, *"All the King's Men* and the Shadow of William James." Reprinted in Clark, *Critical Essays on Robert Penn Warren*, 160-71.

42. "Little Gidding," in Eliot's *Complete Poetry and Plays, 1909-1950* (New York: Harcourt, Brace & World, 1971), 142-43.

43. The novel's epigraph, from Canto III of the *Purgatorio*, is obviously an important key, as numerous readers have noted. Those familiar with the voluminous body of commentary on *All the King's Men* will recognize my particular debt throughout to Norton R. Girault's fine pioneering article "The Narrator's Mind as Symbol: An Analysis of *All the King's Men*,"

Accent 7 (1947): 220-34. Reprinted in Robert H. Chambers, ed., *Twentieth Century Interpretations of* All the King's Men (Englewood Cliffs, N.J.: Prentice-Hall, 1977).

44. Guttenberg, *Web of Being*, 38, and Richard G. Law ("The Nature of Truth in *All the King's Men*," in Bloom, *Robert Penn Warren's* All the King's Men, 142) note the relationship between *All the King's Men* and Warren's famous study of Coleridge's *Ancient Mariner*, "A Poem of Pure Imagination" (1946) in *Selected Essays*, 198-305. Like the Mariner, Jack learns through suffering that "love" is the defining force behind a redeemed vision. For a seminal investigation of the relationship between Coleridge's Mariner and the embedded narratives in Warren's fiction, see James H. Justus, "The Mariner and Robert Penn Warren," *Texas Studies in Literature and Language* 8 (1966): 117-28. Also in Clark, *Critical Essays on Robert Penn Warren*, 111-21.

45. In the play *All the King's Men* (New York: Random, 1960), Jack expresses what we must regard as a regressive attitude toward Tiny Duffy: " 'he is nothing, nothing. If he were something. If he were real. If he were human. I would have killed him. But he is nothing. He is the Great Twitch' " (133). I would argue that this latter passage is less an expression of Warren's own attitudes than a concession to "dramatic" conventions, which discourage the philosophical subtleties possible in a novel. Note, however, the parallel attitude of Perse Munn toward Senator Tolliver in *Night Rider* and Duckfoot Blake's insistence that Bogan Murdock is "not real" in *At Heaven's Gate*.

46. "Warren on the Art of Fiction" in Watkins and Hiers, *Robert Penn Warren Talking*, 36.

47. I have traced the process in question at length in "A Meditation on Folk-History: The Dramatic Structure of Robert Penn Warren's *The Ballad of Billie Potts*," *American Literature* 49 (1978): 635-45.

5. Renegotiating the Covenant

1. See my "Warren's Criticism and the Evolving Self," *Kenyon Review* ns 7 (1985): 48-53. Louis D. Rubin, Jr., provides a useful contrast between Warren's approach to criticism and that of certain contemporary theorists in "Robert Penn Warren: Critic," in Edgar, *Southern Renascence Man*, 19-37.

2. Introduction to *Selected Poems of Herman Melville: A Reader's Edition* (New York: Random, 1970), 25.

3. Watkins and Hiers, *Robert Penn Warren Talking*, 22. Subsequent references to this volume appear parenthetically in the text.

4. By the mid-1960s, Warren was explicitly proclaiming his sense of the interrelationship between poetry and the prophetic impulse, as Victor Strandberg rightly notes (*Poetic Vision of Robert Penn Warren*, 272). His published appraisals of Whittier, Hawthorne, Melville, Dreiser, and Twain reveal much about his own assumption of a consciously prophetic

role, as does his collaboration with Cleanth Brooks and R.W.B. Lewis on a magisterial anthology of American writing, *American Literature: The Makers and the Making*, 2 vols. (New York: St. Martin's, 1973). See Lewis's account of Warren's work on that project: "Warren's Long Visit to American Literature," *Yale Review* 70 (1981): 568-591.

5. Without necessarily accepting the ideological imputations that define it, the student of Warren may gain much from Sacvan Bercovitch's influential study *The American Jeremiad* (Madison: Univ. of Wisconsin Press, 1978), especially 180-81.

6. Warren makes this point in "Melville the Poet," *Kenyon Review* 8 (1946): 208-23 (reprinted in the *Selected Essays* of 1958).

7. James Longenbach, *Modernist Poetics of History: Pound, Eliot, and the Sense of the Past* (Princeton: Princeton Univ. Press, 1987), 16.

8. Ibid., 27.

9. Ibid., 149.

10. Ibid., 27.

11. See Walker, *Robert Penn Warren: A Vision Earned*, 109.

12. *The Ballad of Billie Potts* first appeared in the *Partisan Review* in 1944. I am quoting here from the version of the poem included in Warren's *Selected Poems: 1923-1975* (New York: Random, 1976), 273.

13. As is so often the case, the analysis of James H. Justus is invaluable. See *Achievement of Robert Penn Warren*, 223-35. While my reading of *World Enough and Time* parallels that of Justus in the main, I see the narrator in a somewhat different light.

14. *World Enough and Time*, 277. Subsequent references will be handled parenthetically.

15. "Shoes in Rain Jungle," in *Selected Poems: New and Old, 1923-1966* (New York: Random House, 1966), 51. America's involvement in the Vietnam conflict was just getting under way in earnest when Warren wrote this remarkably prescient poem.

16. The tension between sons and fathers and a son's particular need to accept and embrace his father's failings are two of Warren's most persistent motifs, as innumerable commentators have pointed out. Warren's virtual obsession with this relationship clearly points toward a deep personal ambivalence on his part. Warren would seem to have had his last word on this subject in the memoir *Portrait of a Father* (Lexington: Univ. Press of Kentucky, 1988), but a fuller understanding must await the publication of a detailed biography. At this writing, Joseph Blotner is at work on such a project.

17. See Justus, *Achievement of Robert Penn Warren*, 222.

18. Warren remarks: "We have less to fear sometimes from the powers of darkness than from would-be angels of light, and the would-be angels of light change their plumage from time to time. Right now the fashionable cut in wings and haloes is not that of the New Deal" ("Knowledge and the Image of Man," reprinted in Longley, *Robert Penn Warren: A Collection of Critical Essays*, 241).

19. The phrase "dialogic imagination" is, of course, most frequently

associated with the Russian theoretician M.M. Bakhtin. Without applying
the term technically to Warren's work, one can argue that Warren, like
those masters of high modernism Eliot and Pound, was instinctively
drawn to the possibilities (if not the inevitabilities) of "dialogism." See
M.M. Bakhtin, *The Dialogic Imagination: Four Essays*, ed. Michael Hol-
quist (Austin: Univ. of Texas Press, 1981), 426.

20. "'Canaan's Grander Counterfeit': Jefferson and America in *Brother
to Dragons*," *Renascence* 30 (1978): 171-78; reprinted in James A. Grimshaw, Jr., ed., *Robert Penn Warren's* Brother to Dragons: *A Discussion*
(Baton Rouge: Louisiana State Univ. Press, 1983), 144-52. Grimshaw's
collection of reviews, essays, and related materials pertaining to both the
1953 and 1979 versions of the poem is an invaluable resource. See especially Richard G. Law's essay, "*Brother to Dragons:* The Fact of Violence
vs. the Possibility of Love," 125-43.

21. *Brother to Dragons*, 40. All subsequent references will appear in the
text. I am among the minority of Warren scholars who prefer this earlier
version by very reason of its more vigorous *roughness*.

22. For an important discussion of the role of R.P.W. in the poem, see
Dennis M. Dooley's "The Persona R.P.W. in Warren's *Brother to Dragons*,"
included in Grimshaw, *Robert Penn Warren's* Brother to Dragons, 101-11.

23. In *Promises*, 40-41. References to other poems in this volume will
appear in parentheses.

24. Leaving aside for the moment the question of less formalized
methods of discrimination and focusing solely on de jure segregation, it
should be noted that in 1954 twenty-one states *and* Washington, D.C.
maintained legally segregated education systems. See Richard Polenberg,
*One Nation Divisible: Class, Race, and Ethnicity in the United States since
1938* (New York: Penguin, 1980), 153.

25. *Segregation*, n.p. Subsequent references appear in the text.

26. See *The Legacy of the Civil War* (1961; reprint, Cambridge: Harvard
Univ. Press, 1983), especially 71-76, 101-9.

27. Hugh Ruppersburg puts it very well when he observes that *Who
Speaks for the Negro?* represents "Warren's attempt to investigate in the
matrix of contemporary affairs the important themes of his poetry and
fiction: the tension between pragmatism and idealism, free will and
determinism; the meaning of identity, the individual in the modern world,
the burden of history, the future of American democracy." For Warren, the
civil rights movement "compels a personal drama of self-definition." See
Ruppersburg's "Robert Penn Warren and the 'Burden of Our Time': *Segregation* and *Who Speaks for the Negro?*," *Mississippi Quarterly* 42 (1989):
115-28.

28. *Who Speaks for the Negro?* 212-13. Subsequent citations appear
parenthetically in the text.

29. Malcolm X's *Autobiography* reads like the extended "confession" of
a Warren protagonist. Among other things, Malcolm became in prison a
compulsive student, determined to wring every drop of knowledge possible from books. He copied a dictionary by hand, and armed with a new

"word-base" read frenetically: "Anyone who has read a great deal can imagine the new world that opened. Let me tell you something: from then until I left that prison, in every free moment I had, if I was not reading in the library, I was reading on my bunk. You couldn't have gotten me out of books with a wedge" (*The Autobiography of Malcolm X*, as told to Alex Haley [1965; New York: Ballantine Books, 1973], 172-73). Characters like Willie Stark and Jed Tewksbury (*A Place to Come To* [1977]) display strikingly similar behavior.

30. The strange empathy Warren felt for Malcolm X can be seen in his essay-review of the *Autobiography* ("Malcolm X: Mission and Meaning," *Yale Review* 56 [1967]: 161-71]), in which he obviously resists the notion that Malcolm had arrived at a definitive knowledge of the "truth" during his pilgrimage to Mecca. Something of Warren's own skepticism regarding orthodoxies of any kind would seem to inform his attitude here. In the early 1980s, Warren would describe Malcolm X to Edwin Thomas Wood as "one of the most fascinating persons I ever met," and, perhaps significantly, he revealed at that time no need to undercut Malcolm's unqualified praise for Islam ("On Native Soil," 184).

31. Nonetheless, Warren did not always succeed in rising above a simplistic expression of his feelings and an oversimplified treatment of his subject. I would point to the poems "Man in the Street" (from *You, Emperors, and Others* [1960]), "Patriotic Tour and Postulate of Joy" (from *Selected Poems, New and Old* [1966]), and "News Photo" (from *Or Else— Poems/Poems, 1968-1974* [New York: Random, 1974]). Allen Tate voiced strong reservations about the value of this last poem in a letter of Jan. 21, 1966 (Warren Papers). Warren dropped all three poems from the *New and Selected Poems* of 1985, but this may ultimately have been the result of space considerations. A number of his more successful poems are also missing.

32. "Why Do We Read Fiction?" in *New and Selected Essays* (New York: Random, 1989), 64. The original version of this essay dates from the early 1960s.

33. *The Image*, 3. Warren cited *The Image* with obvious approbation in "A Dearth of Heroes," *American Heritage* (Oct. 1972): 99. It might also be worth noting that he suggested in the same essay that Martin Luther King, Jr., was likely to occupy a permanent place in the national "pantheon."

34. The epigraph from Plato was apparently an afterthought, suggested by Warren's Random House editor and old friend Albert Erskine (see Watkins and Hiers, *Robert Penn Warren Talking*, 127). Intentions aside, an intertextual approach to Plato's dialogue and *The Cave* enriches both texts.

35. *The Cave* (New York: Random, 1959), 397.

36. *Cave*, 328.

37. See, for example, McLuhan's frankly neo-Agrarian essay of 1945, "The Southern Quality," reprinted in Eugene McNamara, ed., *The Interior Landscape: The Literary Criticism of Marshall McLuhan* (New York: McGraw-Hill, 1969), 185-209. In a phone conversation with me, Cleanth

Brooks once indicated, not without a measure of good-natured humor, that McLuhan had evolved from a fellow traveler to a turncoat.

38. See Warren's response to a question about McLuhan and his work posed by Marshall Walker in 1974 (Watkins and Hiers, *Robert Penn Warren Talking*, 191). The fact that Warren stubbornly refused to own a television set, a source of amusement to many of his acquaintances, speaks for itself.

39. The classic expression of Warren's doctrine of "separateness" is that dictated by the Scholarly Attorney to Jack Burden at the end of *All the King's Men*. See also Warren's essay "Love and Separateness in Eudora Welty," *Kenyon Review* 6 (1944): 246-59.

40. *Meet Me in the Green Glen* (New York: Random, 1971) was published in the same year as Warren's *Homage to Theodore Dreiser* (New York: Random, 1971), and it is instructive to read the novel as Warren's response to Dreiser's *An American Tragedy*. Though Warren was anything but a determinist, his indictment of the "system" is even more pervasive than Dreiser's. Angelo Passetto's innocence is considerably less problematic than that of Dreiser's protagonist Clyde Griffiths, and in Warren's novel even the ACLU must bear some share of the responsibility for Angelo's execution. Still, the obscure lawyer Leroy Lancaster does emerge as a model for emulation, and in this respect he resembles his fellow attorney Blanding Cottshill, the reluctant activist in *Flood: A Romance of Our Time* (New York: Random, 1964). These men of the *law* embody Warren's conviction that—while no system of laws carries with it an absolute guarantee of justice—there is no realistic hope for justice outside the law.

41. Schlesinger's *The Crisis of Confidence: Ideas, Power and Violence in America* (Boston: Houghton Mifflin, 1969) provides an analysis of American attitudes and institutions that is analogous in many respects to the vision that emerges from Warren's work. There is a most telling difference, however, and this difference points up Warren's stubbornly non-partisan even-handedness, which in turn derived from his visceral aversion to doctrinaire party-lines—of whatever stripe. Schlesinger's jeremiad is a conventional (and predictable) articulation of American liberal presuppositions. I would submit that Warren's attitudes were closer to those of a fellow southerner, Senator J. William Fulbright, whose *The Arrogance of Power* (New York: Random, 1967) repays study as a significant document in the history of American dissent.

42. *Democracy and Poetry*, 31. Other page references appear parenthetically in the text. (Incidentally, Warren cites Boorstin on page 60 of *Democracy and Poetry*.)

43. Of course, Warren recognized that there was both a right and a wrong way of responding to a literary text. We see this in tracing the career of Jed Tewksbury, the protagonist of Warren's last novel, *A Place to Come To* (New York: Random, 1977). An academic superstar, Jed gains initial recognition for an essay written as a way of coming to grips with his first wife's agonizing death from cancer. In time, however, his scholarship and criticism become an exercise in self-evasion, and he abandons the role of engaged reader in favor of becoming a pure "technician." Warren was a

superbly equipped critical technician in his own right, but the degree to which he continued to read literature as a way of reading himself is eloquently revealed in the last book he would publish in his lifetime, the *New and Selected Essays* of 1989.

44. In "Warren's *Audubon:* A Portrait of the Artist," *South Atlantic Quarterly* 81 (1982): 387-98, I provide a detailed reading of the poem and briefly survey earlier commentary.

45. *Audubon: A Vision* (New York: Random, 1969), 32.

46. Letter of RPW to William Bedford Clark, Aug. 3, 1982.

47. *Chief Joseph of the Nez Perce*, 55. *Chief Joseph* originally appeared a year earlier in the *Georgia Review.*

48. I cite the text of the poem as it appears in Warren's *New and Selected Poems*, 36. "New Dawn" was first published in the Nov. 14, 1983 issue of the *New Yorker.*

49. "New Dawn," 33.

50. Quite appropriately, "New Dawn" was dedicated to Hersey, a former colleague of Warren's at Yale, and to the artist Jacob Lawrence.

Postscript

1. The conference resulted in a valuable book, *The* Southern Review *and Modern Literature: 1935-1985*, ed. Lewis P. Simpson, James Olney, and Jo Gulledge (Baton Rouge: Louisiana State Univ. Press, 1988).

2. *Chief Joseph of the Nez Perce*, 63-64.

Index